INTERNATIONAL ENCYCLOPEDIA OF ART

Far Eastern Art

first edition

Charles Doherty

Facts On File, Inc.

INTERNATIONAL ENCYCLOPEDIA OF ART
FAR EASTERN ART

Text copyright © 1997 Charles E. Doherty
Copyright © 1997 Cynthia Parzych Publishing, Inc.
Design, maps, timeline design copyright © 1997 Cynthia Parzych Publishing, Inc.

Facts on File, Inc.
11 Penn Plaza
New York NY 10001-2006

Cataloging-in-Publication Data available on request from
Facts On File, Inc.

Facts on File books are available at special discounts when purchased in bulk quantities
for businesses, associations, institutions or sales promotions. Please call our Special
Sales Department in New York at 212/967-8800 or 800/322-8755.

This is a Mirabel Book produced by:
Cynthia Parzych Publishing, Inc.
648 Broadway
New York, NY 10012

Edited by: Frances Helby
Designed by: Dorchester Typesetting Group Ltd.
Printed and bound in Spain by: Imschoot Graphic Service

Front cover: This is a Japanese No mask made from carved and painted wood in the
eighteenth century.

10 9 8 7 6 5 4 3 2 1

Contents

Introduction 5

1   Art of the Middle East and Persia..10
2   Early Art of India 14
3   Gupta Period Art of India 16
4   Medieval and Early Indo-Islamic Art..................................18
5   Art of the British and Post-Colonial Periods in India.............22
6   Art of Nepal and Tibet...24
7   Neolithic, Bronze Age, Qin and Han Dynasty Art of China.........26
8   Tang and Song Dynasty Art of China 28
9   Ming Dynasty Art of China 30
10 Qing Dynasty Art of China 32
11 Twentieth Century Art of China 34
12 Early Art of Japan 36
13 Later Buddhist and Feudal Art of Japan...............................38
14 Japanese Secular Art 40
15 Meiji Period and Modern Art of Japan 42
16 Art of Korea 44
17 Art of Burma and Thailand 46
18 Art of Cambodia, Vietnam, Laos, Malaysia and Singapore.........48
19 Art of Australia and New Zealand.......................................52
20 Art of Indonesia and Oceania..56

Bibliography 60
Glossary...61
Photo Credits..62
Index 63

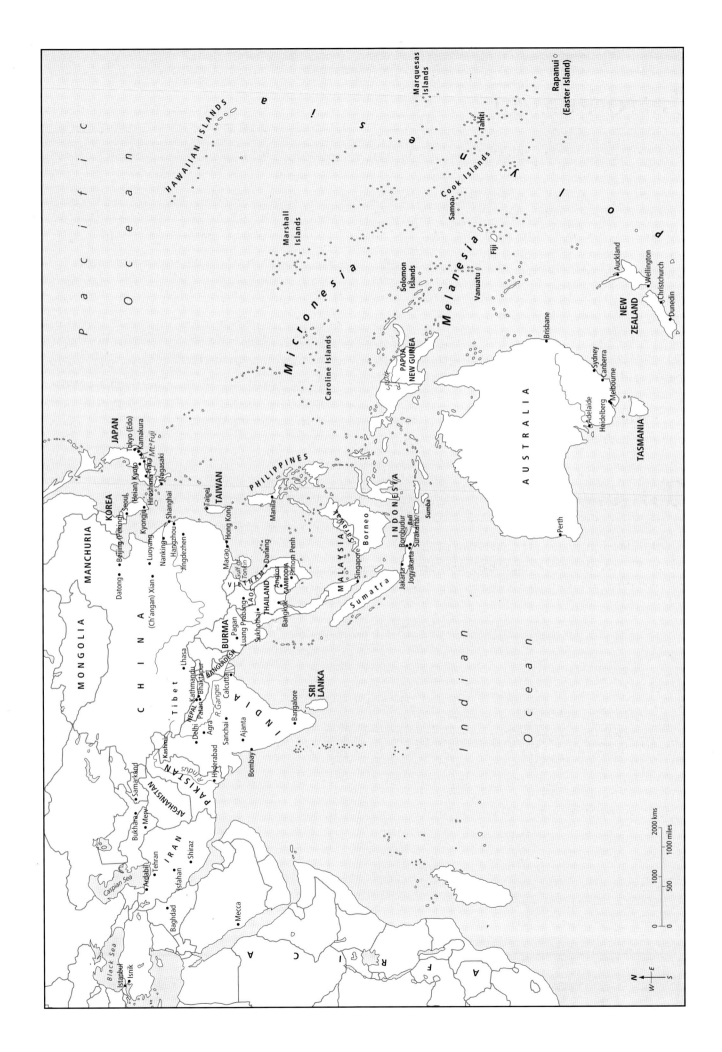

Introduction

The Asian and Australasian continents, along with the islands of the Pacific, form a vast and diverse region. This volume covers the art, history and culture of these continents where over half the world's population live on more than one third of the earth's landmass. The diversity of peoples, geography, religions and history provides a richness unequaled in the rest of the world. This artistic legacy reflects three important influences.

One influence was foreign invasion, trade and missionary work. Without contact with the rest of the world, the art of this great area would have been very different.

Secondly, the many different rulers, including sultans, shahs, shoguns, emperors, tribal chiefs and dictators, have played a key role in shaping the production of art. Rulers, exercising strict control, commissioned artists to develop architecture, paintings and objects in many styles. They have also played a role in the creation of furnishings for temples, mosques, palaces, meeting houses, castles and mausoleums.

The third influence is the interplay of religions which has significantly shaped art production. Islam, Buddhism and Hinduism are the major religions in the region. Each religion evolved locally with variations or into separate religious sects. This complexity has inspired artists to portray a splendid array of gods, goddesses and cult figures in their own manner.

Timeline

This timeline lists some of the important events, both historical (listed above the time bar) and art historical (below) that have been mentioned in this book. While every event cannot be mentioned it is hoped that this diagram will help the reader to understand at a glance how these events relate in time.

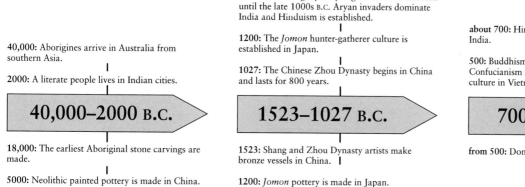

40,000: Aborigines arrive in Australia from southern Asia.

2000: A literate people lives in Indian cities.

40,000–2000 B.C.

18,000: The earliest Aboriginal stone carvings are made.

5000: Neolithic painted pottery is made in China.

1523: The Shang Dynasty begins in China and lasts until the late 1000s B.C. Aryan invaders dominate India and Hinduism is established.

1200: The *Jomon* hunter-gatherer culture is established in Japan.

1027: The Chinese Zhou Dynasty begins in China and lasts for 800 years.

1523–1027 B.C.

1523: Shang and Zhou Dynasty artists make bronze vessels in China.

1200: *Jomon* pottery is made in Japan.

about 700: Hinduism becomes a major force in India.

500: Buddhism is founded in India. Taoism and Confucianism are founded in China. The Dongson culture in Vietnam continues for 300 years.

700–300 B.C.

from 500: Dongson drums are made in Vietnam.

The Middle East and Persian regions stretch from the Arabian Peninsula and Iraq eastward to the western border of China. This is a huge area which fell under Persian influence. This 6,500-mile/more than 10,000 kilometer distance encompasses many of the significant religious sites of Islam. Islam began in the Arabian desert in the early seventh century A.D. It spread gradually eastward over the next 250 years. Virtually all the Middle Eastern and Persian arts and crafts have been, and still are, strongly influenced by Islam. The unified appearance of all sacred and secular art forms shows the great power of Islam in all aspects of daily life.

India is the largest country in southern Asia, running, like an inverted triangle, some 2,900 kilometers (1,800 miles) from the Himalayan mountains in the north to the Indian Ocean in the south. It consists of twenty-four separate states which have richly diverse cultures. Only China has a larger population than India. India has been home to many religions, cultures, and ethnic groups who followed their own artistic, musical and dance traditions.

Nepal and Tibet, in the Himalayas, have historic and cultural links with neighboring China and India. This mountainous, land-locked region became a religious crossroads when Buddhism and Hinduism were spreading north from India. Its geography contributes to the almost unchanging nature of Nepalese and Tibetan art over the centuries. Tibet was taken over by the People's Republic of China in 1959 and many Tibetan refugees fled to Nepal, creating additional ties within the region. Today Nepal serves as an vital center for maintaining Tibetan art and cultural traditions.

Over the past 3,000 years Chinese art has evolved slowly, reflecting subtle changes in a civilization that covers a vast region. Its geographic boundaries and language have changed little, and

---

300: The settled rice growing Yagoi culture in Japan continues for more than 500 years and Shintoism develops.

221–207 B.C.: The Qin Dynasty unifies China, the Great Wall is built and writing and bureaucracy are standardized.

206: The Han Dynasty in China begins and there is a 400 year period of expansion and foreign trade in China.

about 100: The Silk Road is established.

300 B.C.–99 A.D.

from 300: The Yagoi culture allows artists and craftsmen to specialize in Japan.

from 206: Han pottery and jade tomb objects are made in China.

100: The Champa Kingdoms are established in Vietnam and survive until 1720.

200s: Buddhism reaches China.

320: The 300 year Gupta period begins in India.

400s: Over the next 300 years Hindu kingdoms are established throughout southeast Asia.

100–499 A.D.

320: Gupta Hindu and Buddhist religious art is made throughout India.

500s: Chinese writing and bureaucracy are adopted in Japan and history can now be recorded. Buddhism and Shintoism coexist in Japan.

about 570: Mohammed is born and founds Islam.

618: The 300 year Tang Dynasty begins in China and Buddhism becomes increasingly important.

after 647: Hinduism drives Buddhism from India.

688: The Unified Silla period in Korea begins and continues for nearly 300 years.

500–799 A.D.

from 618: Tang religious art and tomb figures are made in China.

from 688: Sculpture and jewelry are made in Korea.

the desire for pottery, paintings and sculpture based upon works of previous eras has remained nearly constant. The continuity of Chinese art mirrors the constancy of the language and institutions that have changed little over nearly thirty centuries. Today, China is the most populous country in the world.

The island nation of Japan was cut off from the culture of its east Asian neighbors for much of its history. Before the sixth century A.D., the only foreign influence and art that came from abroad was from Korea. Few Japanese artists traveled overseas before the late nineteenth century, so the semi-isolated country developed art forms with strong national characteristics. The geographic features of the five islands of Japan played an important role in shaping its art and culture. Because much of the country is susceptible to earthquakes, typhoons, tidal waves, landslides and fires, much of Japanese architecture lacks permanence. There is no native

hard stone, so wooden structures were built that could easily be replaced following a catastrophe. Rooms were divided by paper-covered screens and furnished with small, replaceable objects. Paper, wood and lacquer play more important roles in Japanese culture than in any other.

Korea occupies a peninsula that has a long border with China in the north and juts into the Sea of Japan in the south. Locked between the two strong countries of China and Japan, Korea has always been in the path of invaders, traders and missionaries and this has been important in shaping Korean art and culture. For centuries, Korea has also served as an important transmitter of cultural influences within north Asia.

Burma, now officially called Myanmar, and Thailand, which was once known as Siam, border each other in southeast Asia. Burma, the larger of the two, is half rainforest, half lowland. It is divided from north to south by the long Irrawaddy

---

700: Over the next 500 years Kathmandu, Patan and Bhaktapur become important cities in Nepal where Hinduism and Buddhism coexist.

710: The Japanese capital is established at Nara.

794: Heian is established as the Japanese capital. The Heian period lasts for 400 years.

700–799 A.D.

from 700: Wooden sculpture and architectural carvings are made in Nepal. Nepalese Buddhist manuscript illustrations are made on palm leaves and heavily influenced by Tibetan and Chinese art.

from 794: Heian period temples, shrines and sculpture in wood, bronze and lacquer are made in Japan.

800: The Maoris arrive in New Zealand from Polynesia. Islam begins to penetrate India. The Angkor period begins in Cambodia and survives for 600 years.

935: The Korean Koryo period begins and lasts until 1392.

960: The Song Dynasty begins in China and survives until 1279.

800–999 A.D.

874: Persian art for the next 250 years shows a mixture of Islamic and Chinese influences.

from 960: Song art shows an awareness of Chinese national identity. Art manuals are written and art moves away from naturalism. Some of the finest Chinese painting and porcelain is produced.

---

by 1000: Great Hindu temples are built in India.

1044: Pagan is the capital of Burma until its overthrow by the Mongols in 1287.

1100s: Japan suffers a series of civil wars.

1185: The 200 year Kamakura period begins in Japan.

1190: Genghis Khan begins to build the Mongol Empire.

1199: The first mosque is built in India, as many Hindu and Buddhist temples are destroyed.

1000–1199 A.D.

from 1044: Pagan period architects and artists produce great Burmese architecture and frescoes.

1100s: The Angkor Wat temple complex is built in Cambodia.

from 1185: The Kamakura period is a time of military culture. Armor and swords are intricately decorated and warlords have their portraits painted. No dramas develop.

River. Its fertile valley has been a life-giving force for centuries, like the Nile River in Egypt. Thailand lies to the east of Burma and is mountainous and tropical. Burma and Thailand are on the cultural crossroads between India, China and the countries of southeast Asia. Both Burmese and Thai culture were heavily influenced by Hinduism and Buddhism. These religious influences came from India, Indonesia, Cambodia and Sri Lanka. Burmese culture also had a major influence on neighboring Thailand.

Thailand's neighbor to the east, Cambodia, had widespread trade with India. Indian astrology, architecture, classical literature and dance, as well as Hinduism and its associated religious cults, all left their mark upon many aspects of life. Cambodia itself became an influential force in southeast Asia between the ninth and fourteenth centuries A.D. This was the golden age of Cambodian art, the Angkor period, when Cambodia's architectural compounds with their ornate sculptural decoration were built.

Vietnam and Laos are long, narrow countries in southeast Asia. Historically, they have been dominated by their more powerful Chinese neighbors to the north and by western powers, particularly France and the United States. Most Vietnamese and Laotian cities and towns have been ransacked over the centuries and much early wooden architecture has not survived. However, Thai, Burmese and Cambodian influences are visible in the surviving Buddhist temples and the small art objects used in worship.

Australia and New Zealand are two countries with similar histories. Both have native cultures: Aborigine in Australia and Maori in New Zealand. Prior to the arrival of British colonists in the eighteenth and nineteenth centuries these native cultures thrived. Each indigenous culture produced lively and colorful work based upon ties with

---

1220: The Mongols rule Persia.

1260: The Mongol Yuan Dynasty begins in China and survives for 100 years.

1368: The 300 year Chinese Ming Dynasty begins. It is a time of prosperity.

1369: Timur the Lame sets up his capital at Samarkand.

1392: The Muromatu period begins in Japan. Zen Buddhism is predominant and the tea ceremony develops.

1200–1399 A.D.

from 1220: Persian art shows increasing Chinese influences.

late 1200s: A distinct Thai style of art develops.

from 1368: Cobalt is imported into China from Persia and ceramics can now be decorated in blue.

from 1392: Muromatu period artists emphasize ink painting and calligraphy in Japan.

1446: The Korean alphabet is invented.

1500s: Westerners trade with China for tea, silk and porcelain.

1526: The Mughal Empire is established in India and will last until 1857.

1527: Islam reaches Indonesia.

1400–1572 A.D.

1400s: Persian miniatures reach their height.

1500s: Chinese blue and white porcelain begins to have a long term influence on European ceramics. Persian architecture and pottery become increasingly ostentatious.

1573: The forty year Momayama period begins in Japan.

1592: Japan invades Korea.

from 1600: Secular urban culture in Japan becomes increasingly important. The British begin to come to India and set up trade.

1615: The Edo period brings renewed isolation to Japan that lasts for 200 years.

1644: The Manchu Qing Dynasty in China is established and lasts until 1911.

1788: Colonization of Australia begins.

1573–1799 A.D.

late 1500s: Miniature painting in Mughal India is increasingly important and heavily influenced by Persian miniatures.

after 1592: Many artists are brought to Japan from Korea after the Japanese invasion.

from 1615: Japanese art begins to be made for the merchant class. The *kabuki* theater and *ukiyo-e* prints flourish.

1632: The Taj Mahal is begun in India and takes twenty years to complete.

ancestors and the spirit world. Since Australia and New Zealand became British territories in the nineteenth century, most of the art produced there has reflected British colonial influence.

The southeast Asian republic of Indonesia comprises 13,677 islands, making it the world's largest archipelago. The islands, with their volcanoes and tropical rainforests, stretch along the equator over an area of almost 772,200 square miles/2 million square kilometers. Indonesia is the fourth most populous nation in the world. The major island, Java, is the world's most densely populated area. Indonesians are followers of all the religions of Islam, Christianity, Buddhism and Hinduism, and they speak 583 different languages and dialects and are divided into 300 ethnic groups. This geographic, religious and linguistic diversity contributes to the richness of Indonesian art and culture.

Oceania includes hundreds of islands in the Pacific Ocean, scattered within a triangle bounded by New Guinea in the west, Hawaii in the north and New Zealand in the south. These islands contain many species of tropical flora and fauna. Their art forms and cultural traditions show that imported southeast Asian styles have fused with native, island styles. Carved and woven objects, primarily used during social and religious ceremonies are the works made by Oceanic artists.

The wealth of customs, traditions, rituals and ceremonies in all these regions have shaped art and craft designs for centuries. Great changes, however, are underway. Rapid improvements in communications, transport networks and both internal and external investment projects have modernized great areas. The economic development now in progress is transforming traditional societies and customs, leading to alternative art forms and practices. Future artists will no doubt integrate the wealth of past art traditions into new and exciting work.

1837: Colonization of New Zealand begins.

late 1800s: The central Asian states fall into the hands of Russia.

1867: The Meiji restoration period begins in Japan. Feudalism and Samurai power are abolished and westernization proceeds.

1887: French Indo-China is established to include Cambodia, Vietnam and Laos.

1800–1899 A.D.

1800s: Art throughout Asia, Australasia and Oceania is increasingly influenced by the west as colonial rule makes itself felt. Asian art is influential in the west but settlers in Australasia and Oceania look only to western art.

1910: Rapid changes of the Meiji restoration period create disruption in Japanese society. Nationalism asserts itself in the annexation of Korea in 1910 and incursions into China in the 1930s.

1920: The central Asian states become part of the former U.S.S.R.

1939: World War II begins.

1945: Atomic bombs are dropped on Hiroshima and Nagasaki in Japan. Japan surrenders and World War II ends.

1900–1945 A.D.

early 1900s: Western influences in art are sometime welcomed and absorbed and sometimes rejected. The west begins to have a limited appreciation of the art of Australasia and Oceania.

1947: India, Pakistan, Laos and Indonesia become independent.

1949: After three years of civil war, Mao Zedong leads the Communists to power in China.

1950: Korea is partitioned after a three year war.

1959: The Chinese annex Tibet.

1965: The four year Cultural Revolution begins in China. The Vietnam War starts.

1976: Pol Pot and the Khmer Rouge begin to rule Cambodia for four years.

1945 A.D.–present

from 1945: Post-war Japanese design becomes influential in western art and design. There is a resurgence of interest and pride in native art styles throughout Asia, Australasia and Oceania. In some countries repressive governments control the production of art. The Cultural Revolution in China and Pol Pot's regime in Cambodia destroy lives, culture and art.

1 Art of the Middle East and Persia

Most people in the Middle East and Persia are Muslim. They meet regularly in large buildings called mosques. There are three major parts to the design of a mosque: three arcades or covered walkways, a large quadrangle and a minaret, or tall, thin tower. A mosque official, the *muezzin*, calls worshippers to prayer five times a day from the minaret. Mosques are important religious, educational and social centers, containing schools, libraries and sometimes a hostel for pilgrims.

Mosques are richly decorated with carpets,

Islam

The Muslim religion, Islam, was founded by the Prophet Mohammed (approx. 570–632 A.D.). Mohammed was born in Mecca, Saudi Arabia. After 610, he received revelations from Allah, whom all Muslims worship as the one true god. The revelations were recorded in the Muslim holy book, the Koran. Today, Islam is the second largest religion in the world, and is an influential political and social force in the Middle East, North Africa, Pakistan, Indonesia and Malaysia. ■

ceramics, mosaics, relief carvings and glass and metal lamps. Muslims always face Mecca, the birthplace of Mohammed, when they pray, and mosques throughout the world contain a *mihrab*, a focal point which shows them the direction they must face.

The Silk Road was an important force uniting the region. After 100 B.C., silk and, later, porcelain from China were brought along this major east-west route. Gold, silver, gems and ivory were carried on it eastward.

Persian art from the period from 874 to 1220 A.D. is a rich combination of native and

▲ *Begun in Kell, the Masjid-i-Shah Mosque, commissioned by Shah Abbas I, was completed at Isfahan in 1629. Its beautiful dome is elaborately decorated with multi-colored glazed tiles.*

The Silk Road

The Silk Road was the overland trading route across central Asia that stretched 6,250 miles/10,000 kilometers from China to the Mediterranean. Goods were usually transported in stages by camel caravans which were threatened by attack and sandstorms. In the sixteenth century, European trading ships made this long journey unnecessary. ■

▲ *This bronze jug is inlaid with silver and gold geometric and floral ornament. It dates about 1376 to 1404. Representation of animal or human forms by artists is not allowed by Islamic law.*

▲ *In 1434, Tamerlane commissioned a beautifully designed mausoleum to symbolize the majesty of his reign. The use of decorative tiles on the exterior walls and a new bulbous dome established styles that were popular for centuries afterwards.*

Islamic Ornament

Islamic teaching does not allow artists to represent living forms, either animal or human in religious art. Most of the design elements in Islamic paintings, carpets and architectural decoration are geometric or floral patterns. ■

foreign styles from both the Islamic and Chinese worlds. This is best seen in metalwork, manuscript illuminations and architectural decoration. The Samanids ruled in the area around Bukhara between 874 and 999, producing some of the finest metalwork, including elaborate silver objects.

Trade along the Silk Road provided contact among different cultures and a vital link for art and design styles. The cities of Bukhara, Samarkand and Merv, along with small independent states in central Asia, flourished from the ninth to the sixteenth centuries. They grew rich collecting taxes from travelers crossing their territory. Various societies along the Silk Road absorbed foreign manners and customs. The central Asian population today still reflects this mix of cultures with ethnic Iranians, Mongols, Tajiks, Uzbeks, Turkmens, Afghans, Persians, Jews, Arabs, Chinese and Russians all living in the region.

After about 1220, under Mongol rule, Persian artists were exposed to more Chinese-related designs. The lotus and chrysanthemum were two floral designs well suited to Islamic ornament in porcelain and tile designs for mosques. A great campaign to build more mosques began; decorative tiles, mosaics and stucco relief grew more lavish.

By the fourteenth century, Samarkand was filled with garden pavilions, elaborately decorated with frescoes and richly painted tiles. This was largely due to the famous Mongol conqueror, Timur the Lame, usually called Tamerlane (1336–1405). He established his capital at Samarkand after 1369, and ruled a vast empire stretching from the Mediterranean to Mongolia. Tamerlane was an important patron of

The Mongol Invasion

Invaders swept down from Mongolia after 1206. They reached northern China under Genghis Khan (approx. 1162–1227). In 1219, they overthrew the Shah of Afghanistan and Iran. Their conquests continued under Genghis's grandson Kublai Khan (1260–94) who became the first emperor of the Yuan Dynasty in China. He encouraged Buddhism and used the Silk Road for communications. His empire grew too big, and fell apart, but Mongols still ruled some parts until the late fourteenth century. ■

▲ *This battle scene from a manuscript of 1398 is full of the detailed action, naturalism and drama that characterizes Persian book illustration. The scenes, like this one, often look as if they were viewed from a cliffside or a dramatic angle.*

The Ottoman Empire

The Islamic, Ottoman Empire which lasted over 600 years was centered in what is now Turkey. The Ottomans overran the Byzantine Empire and in 1453, made Constantinople their capital, renaming it Istanbul. Their empire included much of North Africa, southeastern Europe and the Middle East. There was a flowering of the arts in the sixteenth century, as a result of the mixture of eastern and western styles, particularly in carpets, tiles, pottery, book illustration, calligraphy and metalwork. The empire began to decline in the nineteenth century and collapsed with the defeat of its ally, Germany, at the end of World War I. ■

architecture and the arts and set a standard for future rulers.

The art of Persian miniatures reached new heights during the fifteenth and sixteenth centuries. A wholly Persian style evolved at the center of production in the city of Shiraz. Brightly colored landscapes and stories told with interacting human figures were common subjects.

The Safavid Dynasty (1501–1736) had a profound influence on the art and culture of Iran, the modern center of Persia. Their greatest ruler, Shah Abbas I, reigned from 1587 to 1629. He was responsible for a massive building campaign in the city of Isfahan. He commissioned the construction of the Masjid-i-Shah mosque, between 1611 and 1629. He also laid out the city center as a polo ground with many surrounding buildings.

Sixteenth and seventeenth century pottery production was also ostentatious. Ceramic ware resembled Chinese porcelain, whose forms were now prevalent in central Asia. In Isfahan, ceramics produced during this period were elaborate and decorative, rather than functional. Ceramic artists of Isfahan imitated and excelled in Chinese blue and white designs.

The rulers of Persia moved their capital from Isfahan to Tehran in 1796. During the nineteenth century, both Russia and Great Britain became their rivals in the region and the glorious period of supremacy was over. The most important art patrons during the nineteenth and twentieth centuries were the shahs, or emperors, of Iran. They presided over a royal complex in Tehran that included the Peacock Throne, used for Persian coronations.

The last Shah of Iran, Mohammed Reza (1919–80), reigned

◄ *Ottoman tiles were square or rectangular and fitted together in groups, like these mosque tiles from Isnik made in about 1562. Mosque wall decorations were usually multi-colored.*

▲ *The artists who painted decorative tiles also produced porcelain vessels, such as this Isnik bowl, made in about 1510.*

The Ardabil Carpet ▶ *is perhaps the largest ever made in Persia. Produced in silk and wool for the mosque of Ismail Shah at Ardabil in 1539 to 1540, it displays outstanding workmanship and intricate designs. There are approximately 340 knots per square inch or over fifty per square centimeter.*

between 1953 and 1979. He advocated pro-western policies and western arts flourished during the 1960s and 1970s when foreign films, art forms and educational methods began to reach the country. The dilution of traditional Iranian culture was not universally welcomed. The monarch was overthrown in 1979 by an Islamic fundamentalist regime led by the Ayatollah Khomeini (approx. 1900–89). Khomeini reinstated the importance of the Koran and Islamic teachings as the basis of society. Many of the western-educated classes, including western-trained artists, fled the country. The artists who remained in Iran concentrate on more traditional Persian subjects but continue to use western oil and acrylic.

Persian Carpets

Many of the finest carpets in the world come from the Middle East. They are usually made from wool and cotton, or sometimes silk, and have intense maroon and blue colors, fine knotting and a soft velvet texture. Traditionally they have fine floral, small geometric and curvilinear designs, sometimes around a central medallion. Up to the mid-nineteenth century, each region had its own characteristic designs and practices, but these distinctions have blurred over the past 150 years. ■

Soviet Rule

Some of the Islamic regions of Central Asia which included the cities of Bukhara and Samarkand, with their splendid urban design and buildings, fell into the hands of the Russians in the late nineteenth century. By 1922, Turkmenistan, Uzbekistan and Tajikistan were part of the Communist U.S.S.R. Under Soviet control, the arts showed Russian social-realist themes of hard-working peasants and factory workers. The states regained their independence after the breakup of the Soviet Union in 1991. ■

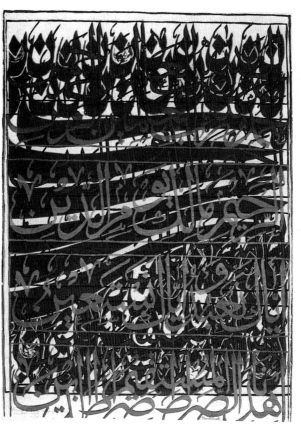

◀ *This modern artist from Iran, Hossein Zenderoudi (1937–) spreads Islamic calligraphy across the entire surface of his graphis works. This is one of his untitled etchings of 1986.*

2 Early Art of India

Aryans and the Aryan Hierarchy

The Aryans were a nomadic people who moved slowly from northwest India towards the Ganges River Valley in the east. Even as early as 1,500 B.C., they had developed a sophisticated hierarchy with a class of rulers, called rajahs, and priests known as brahmins. This hierarchy became the basis for the caste system, so important in India today. This system decides a person's status or class in a society by his or her birth. ■

▲ *Rock-cut caves served as important places of worship for early followers of Buddhism. Sometimes these sanctuaries were carved into the side of a huge boulder or a mountainside. The oldest cave site is at Ajanta in western India. The walls of the thirty caves provide a significant display of Indian Buddhist imagery up to the time the religion was overtaken by Hinduism. The Ajanta caves were used for both Hindu and Buddhist worship between 200 B.C. and 700 A.D. This entrance façade was constructed about 400 A.D. and was pierced by a huge window, letting light into the long worship hall.*

People were living along the semi-fertile Indus River valley three to four thousand years ago. There were elaborately planned cities in this part of northeastern Indian for more than a thousand years. Their ancient inhabitants traded with the civilizations of Mesopotamia and Sumeria. Their sophisticated written language was based on hiero-glyphic symbols. This language has not been completely deciphered in modern times. It appears in inscriptions found on carefully made soapstone cylinder seals like those made by the Sumerians and Akkadians.

Scientific analysis of pottery excavated from ancient villages has made it possible to date the civilization. The ceramics have pure lines and simple decorations with stylized animals and plant forms. Sculpture was produced on a small scale using bronze, sandstone, soap-stone and limestone. These materials were used by Indian artists to make sculpture for many centuries. Some figures resemble those of ancient Sumeria, while others evolved into a purely Indian style. Some folk art figurines made in terracotta represent mother-goddesses, while others depict small Indian animals.

The arrival of the nomadic Aryan peoples who lived further west, after 1,800 B.C., led to a shift in civilization from the Indus Valley to other areas of the Indian subcontinent. The Aryans began to settle and intermingle with the local cultures, bringing their own rituals to various parts of India. Their religious beliefs are recorded in sacred hymns known as Vedas, which means "knowledge." The Vedas were written in the ancient Sanskrit language. Powerful forces of nature, including Indra, the god of thunder and rain; Surya, the sun god; and

The Beginnings of Buddhism

Buddhism has been the most widespread religion in Asia, affecting almost every region. Today, nearly half the world's population lives in a country influenced by Buddhism. It began in India between 600 and 500 B.C. and flourished there for its first thousand years. Prince Siddhartha Gautama (approx. 563–approx. 483 B.C.) was its founder. He achieved "enlightenment", or everlasting life, and became known as the Buddha, the Enlightened One. Everyone could follow his path by leading a life of moderation based on a strong moral code. Buddhism spread along the Silk Road and beyond, and became a major force throughout Asia, though it declined in India in the seventh century. ■

This first century A.D. *tree goddess is called a bracket figure. This is because the figure looks like a bracket supporting the arm of a gateway. The goddess is supposed to bring prosperity to humanity, like a tree bearing fruit.*

Gestures and Symbols in Buddhism

There are many ways of portraying the Buddha, sometimes sitting, sometimes standing. His hand gestures and posture indicate his different roles. Buddhism has many symbols: the Bodhi Tree under which the Buddha was meditating when he attained Enlightenment; the bodhisattva, an Enlightened being dedicated to bringing others to Enlightenment; the lotus flower symbolizing Mount Meru, the home of the gods; and snake kings, which represent the gods, guardians of land and water and which later evolved into serpent and dragon symbols. ■

The Sri Lankan Style

Before 1972, the island of Sri Lanka was called Ceylon. A traditional form of Buddhism was practiced there from before the third century A.D. After the fourth century, Buddhism was exported from here to Thailand and Burma. The simple, sensuous Buddhas of Sri Lanka are defined by a wide face, powerful jaw and characteristic long earlobes. ■

Agni, the god of fire were worshipped by the Aryans.

The early inhabitants of India had two styles of architecture. The first, called a *chaitya*, was a cave-temple cut into the side of a large rock. It was decorated with broad expanses of relief carvings and pillars with carved capitals. The second style, in stone or rock, imitates structures made of timber. These buildings look as though they were put together with nails or interlocking joints, as if they were made of wood, yet they are solid stone. This basic style and appearance persisted in Indian architecture for many centuries.

Each of these architectural styles was used later by the early Buddhists for their temples and stupas. A stupa is a mounded dome of earth supported by a square base where relics or keepsakes associated with the Buddha are kept. Sometimes a stupa may appear as a cylindrical column, resembling a plump rocketship. These were built in the first century A.D. in the ancient kingdom of Gandhara, in modern Pakistan.

Sculpture is the most outstanding art form produced between the first and the fourth centuries A.D. The free-standing sculpture and narrative relief carvings are lifelike and full of vitality. Art from different areas of the Indian subcontinent shows that there was contact with various outside cultures. For example, the figures in Gandhara confirm the influence of Hellenistic Greece, the culture that flourished in the Mediterranean region of Europe and North Africa. Gandhara figures have straight noses and narrow mustaches, they wear garments with drapery folds like those of ancient Greece.

◀ *This bodhisattva, carved in schist about 150–200 at Gandhara, is lifelike and full of energy. The handsome face may be a portrait produced from real life. The figure has intricately arranged long hair. The work shows the influence of Hellenistic Greek sculpture, particularly in the carving of the folds of the clothing.*

3 | Gupta Period Art of India

Hinduism existed in India as early as 1500 B.C., although never a potent force until after 700 B.C. Unlike most other Asian religions, Hinduism lacks a single founder, a single prophet, a single god or even a single set of fixed beliefs. Hindus worship in their homes or more elaborately in temples.

The Hindu temple is a symbolic representation of the universe. The outside walls are filled with stories of gods, men, animals and plant forms. Generally the temple is square in shape. One of the earliest is at Sanchai. Two smaller stupas surround The Great Stupa and they all date between the third century B.C. and the first century A.D. The large mounds probably once held relics of the Buddha. Nearby were four ceremonial entrance gates,

▲ This is the Great Stupa at Sanchai. Built between the third century B.C. and the first century A.D., it is the oldest Hindu temple.

▲ This is the north gate, one of four ceremonial gates near the Great Stupa at Sanchai. It was carved in sandstone by ivory carvers from the nearby town of Benhnagar with figures that are rich in symbolism. It measures thirty-four feet/more than ten meters in height.

Vishnu

Vishnu is the great Hindu savior, protecting all the people in the world. He is usually shown with a human face, but in one of his ten animal incarnations. In Hindu tales, he reappeared as a fish, a tortoise or a boar, in order to rescue the world from various impending disasters. ■

◄ Some Hindus worship Shiva as the supreme, destroyer god. He often appears with multiple arms, holding a drum that symbolizes creation and a circle of flames that symbolizes destruction. He is also known as the Lord of the Dance, and is often shown with one leg raised in a sacred dance, as in this eleventh-century bronze statue.

The Gupta Period

The Gupta period (320–647 A.D.) was the first golden age in Indian history, when the northeastern Gupta rulers controlled a vast part of northern and central India. This period was at its height in the fourth and fifth centuries before the arrival of the invading Huns. They were a nomadic people from the Volga, in modern Russia, who had already invaded the Roman Empire. ■

▲ *Ganesha, the half-man, half-elephant deity is one of the most popular in India. He is usually represented as pot-bellied and holding a bowl of candy, as in this stone carving. Today meetings, family gatherings and inaugurations of buildings begin with prayers to the prosperity-bringing god. This figure of Ganesha was carved in schist in about the thirteenth century.*

covered with Buddhist and Hindu carvings.

The oldest Hindu scriptures are the Vedas, based on Aryan hymns. From these stories emerged three major gods who are widely worshipped by Hindus: Brahma, Shiva and Vishnu. Generally, Hindus conduct their worship in a temple dedicated to one of the three gods.

There are many Hindu festivals throughout the year. Most of the worship is conducted in temples whose outer walls are covered in vast displays of three-dimensional sculpture and relief carvings. These carvings were derived from the myths associated with the glorification of a particular god. Many symbolic carvings were used to illustrate these myths: figures of women represented abundance, embracing couples symbolized prosperity and clusters of foliage suggested growth.

Many other Hindu gods are worshiped. They include Shakti and Ganesha. The mother-goddess Shakti was famous for her battle with a giant demon. She is often depicted in sculptures and paintings with a sword in one hand and the severed head of the giant in the other. Ganesha, the son of Shiva, is one of the most popular gods. He has the head of an elephant and the body of a pot-bellied human being. He brings prosperity because he removes all the obstacles in life and makes things happen.

Between the fourth and the seventh centuries A.D., Hindu kingdoms sprang up throughout southeast Asia as foreign trade linked India with Burma, Malaysia and Indonesia. It was during this time, known as the Gupta period, that Hinduism, along with Indian civilization as a whole, became a vital force throughout much of Asia.

During the Gupta period, artists produced a wide range of Hindu and Buddhist religious works. Hindu art, in particular, flourished. All art forms and philosophic thought expanded under Hindu teachings. Music and dance had particular significance in shaping the religious life of the region. Poems, dramas, fables and epics sprang up across the subcontinent, written first in Sanskrit and later in regional languages. They, too, were important for the spread of Hinduism to other parts of southeast Asia. The *Ramayana* and the *Mahabharata* are just two of these fabled dance-dramas of Indian culture that have been portrayed in Asian painting and sculpture for centuries.

Two Famous Dance Dramas

The *Ramayana* and the *Mahabharata*, two Hindu dance dramas, date between the second century B.C. and the first century A.D. The *Ramayana* has more than 24,000 verses. It takes a week to perform and is about Rama who tries to rescue his kidnapped wife. The *Mahabharata* which is about the trials of two rival families, has 90,000 stanzas. ■

4 Medieval and Early Indo-Islamic Art

Islam in India_____

Islam spread to northern India during the Arab conquests of the seventh and eighth centuries. It eventually spread throughout the subcontinent in the thirteenth and fourteenth centuries and is today a vital religious force in parts of northern India and Pakistan. ■

This is a ▶ *bronze figure of Parvati, the consort of Shiva, cast in bronze in southern India in the tenth century. The delicacy of the garment that clings to the figure's legs shows the great skill of the artist. Although bronze is a heavy material, this graceful figure appears lighter because of its elegant design.*

After the fall of the Gupta dynasty in 647, powerful, yet fragmented kingdoms controlled the Indian subcontinent. Buddhism virtually disappeared in most of India. Hinduism became the predominant religion, coexisting with Islam after the eighth century. Islam arrived in western India first, from the Arab peninsula via Persia, reaching what is now Pakistan and then slowly advancing to the east. By the twelfth and thirteenth centuries it had reached northern and central India. Temple design, sculpture, and paintings reflect the coexistence of Hindu and Islamic art forms.

Great Hindu temples were built during the Middle Ages. By the year 1000 there were two types. The *vimana,* in the south, was a square temple with a pyramid-shaped roof with steps, like the pyramids of the Old Kingdom of ancient Egypt. The northern type, called *sikhara,* was also square-shaped with a pyramidal roof that curved inward. Both types were set in walled complexes with monumental gateways that took on gigantic proportions between the fourteenth and the sixteenth centuries.

At this time, low-relief carving and free-standing figures decorated Hindu temples and gateways. Low-relief carving became very elaborate and began to cover entire walls. Free-standing figures included single figures or loving couples. Many appear as religious sculpture in

The Mughal Rulers_____

The first Mughal emperor, Babur (1483–1530) invaded northern India in 1526. In his four-year reign, he established the Mughal traditions of poetry, literature and art. His grandson, Akbar the Great, controlled all northern India. He established uniform laws and administrative procedures and advocated religious tolerance. He was a cosmopolitan ruler who welcomed Jesuit priests, hung European paintings on the palace walls and laid great emphasis on philosophical thought. He inspired his artists to include landscape vistas, western perspective and the atmospheric components of mist, daylight and twilight from European paintings in their work. Akbar's sons, Jahangir and Shah Jahan, succeeded him. They reigned in a time of peace and prosperity. Both were patrons of the arts. In the eighteenth century, Mughal rule began to weaken as regional interests destabilized it. The British East India Company became a political force and the British deposed the last Mughal king in 1857. ■

The Q'utb ▶ Minar minaret of the oldest mosque in India rises to 240 feet/seventy-three meters and dominates the skyline. It is the tallest minaret in India. Local Hindu craftsmen from Delhi, where the minaret is located, created the beautiful carvings on the stonework. Their carving can be found everywhere in the city of Delhi.

temples, made in stone or bronze. The greatest cast-bronze figures appeared in southern India during the tenth and eleventh centuries.

The arrival of Islam in central India had a huge impact. Islamic invaders destroyed many Buddhist and Hindu sculptures and temples, and built in their place vast mosques for the worship of Allah. Unlike the Hindu temple's human sculptures, traditional Islamic mosques used only geometric and abstract patterns for surface decoration.

The first mosque in India was the Q'utb Minar complex in Delhi begun in 1199. It was built using fragments of destroyed Hindu temples. The mosque and its minaret were conceived as a towering monument to the Islamic conquest of the non-believers. The complex combines aspects of Persian mosque design with native Indian elements. The Q'utb Minar minaret served as the prototype for minarets throughout India.

A glorious period in Indian art and culture began in 1526 with the arrival of the Muslim Mughal emperors. Islamic painting reached great heights. Glassware, metalwork and carpet weaving also flourished.

Akbar the Great (1542–1605) established a new school of painting under the direction of two master painters from the Safavid court in Persia. They trained Indian artists to produce small Persian-style miniatures as illustrations for manuscripts.

Perhaps the most famous manuscript to combine Persian and Indian elements is the *Hamza-Nama*. Commissioned early in Akbar's reign, the illustrated manuscript included 1,400 miniature paintings

Indian Miniatures and Persian Influence

Indian miniatures were made on palm leaves or paper. They attained a new role during the Mughal period through the inspiration of the Persian court painters. Persian paintings looked flat with little sense of spatial depth of foreground and background. They were richly patterned with images of decorative court dress, carpets and other objects. Both Indian and Persian miniatures often include extremely elegant, curving lines in the composition and in the border areas. ■

◀ *This action scene,* Akbar Tames the Savage Elephant, Hawa'i, *outside the Red Fort at Agra, was rendered in bright colored gouache on paper in about 1590. It typifies much of Indian miniature painting. The unusual and awkward angle for viewing the scene was derived from Persian miniatures and intensifies the drama.*

▲ Gardeners Beating the Giant Zamurrud Entrapped in a Well *from the* Hamza-Nama *is one of only 150 paintings to survive from the series of 1,400 produced between 1556 and 1605.*

This detail of a ▶ floral, Mughal carpet, mirrors the designs found in contemporary metalwork, textiles and architectural ornament. It was produced about 1650 when there was much contact with western European merchants and diplomats.

Mughal Portraiture___

Mughal emperors had no difficulty with the Islamic ban on portrayals of the human form. Jahangir and Shah Jahan were influenced by western art and commissioned portraits, historical paintings and other scenes. Painters now studied and recorded accurately the faces of the emperor and his court officials. ■

The Mughal ▶ emperor Jahangir commissioned court artists to produce images of hunting escapades, that were also accurate natural history records, such as this watercolor on paper of about 1610, Squirrels in a Plane Tree.

bound in fourteen volumes. It tells the life-story and adventures, real and imagined, of the Amir Hamza, an uncle of the prophet Mohammed, who traveled through foreign lands in the sixth century, spreading the Islamic faith.

The paintings include strong, hot colors, energetic figures and animals, and realistic details. They all symbolized the supreme rule of the new Mughal emperor, Akbar. He had commissioned an extensive manuscript whose appearance and forceful message would be unmistakably imperial. Its style influenced Mughal painting for the next 200 years.

During the reigns of Jahangir from 1605 to 1627 and Shah Jahan from 1627 to 1658, Indian artists used the same bold colors, outlined forms and painting techniques. But images of exotic natural forms, such as insects, birds and beasts as well as fine imperial portraits, were now added.

Other Arts of the Mughal Period _

Glass blowing, carpet and textile weaving, lacquerware, embroidery, jewelry, metalwork, enameling and carvings in stone, ivory and wood all reached new heights during the seventeenth and eighteenth centuries. Mughal artists incorporated European and Persian designs into their Indian patterns to create new decorative styles. ■

The Mughal Garden and Islam

Islam was born in the desert of the Arabian peninsula. Water and green, growing plants were rarities. In the Koran, a garden is a symbol of paradise, and in Muslim paintings, paradise is represented by a garden. To the Muslim, an enclosed garden is heaven on earth. It is no surprise that green is the symbolic color of Islam and in a mausoleum like the Taj Mahal, the garden is as important as the tomb itself. ■

▲ *The magnificent marble faced Taj Mahal built between 1632 and 1643 seems to change appearance at different times of day. Under early morning mist, midday sun or the soft tones of dusk, it appears to change color. There is an Islamic garden nearby, completed in 1654, representing paradise on earth.*

Rajput painting was popular during the Mughal period. The Rajput clans ruled northwestern and central India between the seventh and thirteenth centuries. Their brightly colored paintings, like this one produced about 1630, are more like folk art, depicting simple stories in a naive manner. Rajput painters generally did not accurately record human anatomy and nature. The style grew from the medieval Indian tradition, and an awareness of Persian miniatures. ▼

Jahangir (1569–1627) was particularly fond of nature, and required his court artists to follow him everywhere, even out hunting. Like a palace photographer in the twentieth century, the painter was a visual scribe following the emperor into the animal kingdom.

Shah Jahan's (1592–1666) greatest commission was the Taj Mahal, the best known building in India. Nearly 125 miles/200 kilometers south of Delhi, it was built between 1632 and 1654 as a loving tribute to the emperor's wife, Mumtaz Mahal. Her name means "Jewel of the Palace" and the memorial emphasizes her prominent role in the empire. The name *Taj-i-mahal* means "The Crown of the Palace." The crown-like domed building along the south bank of the Yumuna River was set in sight of the emperor's enclosed compound.

The Taj Mahal is built of red sandstone faced with white marble. The marble was quarried some 186 miles/300 kilometers away and transported by 1,000 elephants. The grand design, elegant proportions, exquisite craftsmanship and purely Islamic components all contribute to its magnificence. There are four slender minarets balancing the huge dome that dominates the complex. There are decorative calligraphic passages from the Koran, both as inlay work and carving, in the black interior marble. The perfectly proportioned ceiling allows the chants from the Koran to reverberate throughout the space inside.

21

5 Art of the British and Post-Colonial Periods in India

Europeans began to come to India by sea as traders. The British set up their first trading post in the early seventeenth century and their first settlement by 1690. The British eventually used their Indian ports for conducting business all across southeast Asia. They bought Indian cotton and shipped it to

British East India Company _____

The British East India Company was set up in 1600. It sought control over the import of Indian goods to England and Europe. There was competition from the Portuguese, Dutch and French so, during the eighteenth century, the British East India Company established its own empire in India. ■

Kashmir Shawls _____

Woolen shawls were made in Kashmir from about 1420. They were brought to Europe by British traders and after 1770, copied in England and Scotland. The British cloth mills were part of the reason for the collapse of Indian weaving. Most Indian crafts suffered a similar fate under British rule. ■

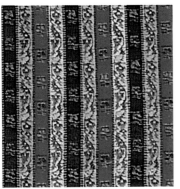

◀ *Making a Kashmir shawl was like weaving a tapestry and could take eighteen months to complete. They were prized gifts during the reign of the Mughal emperors.*

▲ *A young Indian prince (center) poses for this photograph with his advisors and the British political officers (at left in dark uniforms) who were stationed in each of the Indian courts by the British government during the Raj period.*

the Spice Islands in exchange for spices which they brought to Great Britain. Splendid woolen shawls from Kashmir, precious Indian gems and, after 1700, the finest Indian carpets resembling Mughal paintings were also brought back.

Photography in India _____

Photography reached India in the 1840s and was a well established profession by the end of the century. Lin Din Dayal (1844–1910), became a court photographer in Hyderabad in 1884. He portrayed a wide range of Indian subjects, including portraits architectural scenes and panoramic views of elephants, tents and distinguished visitors in caravans. ■

▲ *Mahatma Gandhi, photographed with his two granddaughters in New Delhi, inspired many people throughout the world with his belief in non-violence and peace.*

Modern Indian Art ___

Starting in 1991, Bombay, Bangalore, Calcutta, Delhi and Hyderabad became exciting venues for Indian art with galleries, bohemian bistros and coffee houses displaying contemporary art. Indian art reflects a rich cultural diversity. ■

▲ *Pakistan also has an exciting modern art scene. The Mayo School of Arts in Lahore has produced many successful artists such as Jamil Naqsh (1937–) who painted* Composition *in oil on canvas in 1980.*

Mahatma Gandhi_____

Mahatma Gandhi (1869–1948) was probably the most influential twentieth century Indian leader. He advocated British withdrawal from India and promoted non-violent protest. Although he tried to unite the Hindus and the Muslims, he was assassinated by Hindu extremists on January 30, 1948. ■

Political and economic power began to shift from the Mughals to the British and, as the Mughal Empire declined, the Indian economy fell into ruin with decaying roads and irrigation systems. Gradually, the British built canals, roads, railways and provided English-language education.

Yet, the British found the vast empire politically unmanageable. There was a series of revolts throughout India, usually stopped by military force. The most famous was the Indian Mutiny of 1857 to 1858 and its finish in 1858 marked the end of the Mughal Empire and East India Company rule. From 1858 until 1948, the British government ruled India. This is sometimes referred to as the British Raj period. *Raj* is the Hindi word meaning "rule "or "government."

European artists brought oil and watercolor painting to India. The British organized art schools, often with departments specializing in crafts. The British head of the Calcutta Art School, around 1900, inspired a revival of traditional Indian art subjects and styles.

The assimilation of western and Indian art traditions grew stronger in the 1930s and 1940s. One artist, Amrita Sher Gil (1913–41), studied in Paris and fell under the spell of the French Post-Impressionist painter Paul Gauguin (1848–1903). Her colorful compositions of humble Indian people inspired Indian artists for generations.

Following World War II, there was renewed pressure to partition India along roughly religious lines. The mainly Muslim areas in the northwest and northeast became Pakistan in 1947, the remainder, largely Hindu, became today's India. Problems still arise from this partition. The two parts of Pakistan split into Pakistan and Bangladesh. Kashmir remains a disputed area.

Since independence in 1948, India has struggled with a shaky economy and political system. During the 1950s, a series of five-year plans was developed to improve agriculture and industry. Tight government control, severe limits on foreign investment and restrictions to free enterprise held back India's economic progress.

The Indian government began to relax its restrictive economic policies in 1991. New industries emerged. From the late 1980s Bombay and Delhi made great strides. Exciting architecture and art galleries appeared, while old buildings began to be preserved.

6 Art of Nepal and Tibet

Nepal maintained the Buddhist-Hindu religious duality that died out in India. Early Nepalese wood and brick architecture imitated Indian stupas, but the Nepalese painted four pairs of squinting eyes, their purpose unknown, just above the dome.

Most Nepalese art was produced by the Newar people from the Kathmandu Valley. Between the seventh and the twelfth centuries, the neighboring cities of Kathmandu, Patan and Bhaktapur arose. Each city's central focus was the royal palace. Their surrounding squares included free-standing, red brick temples, stepped platforms and bronze statues. Most of these buildings contain intricate wood sculpture around the doors and windows. The carvings are joined to the brick by "weaving" them into place without the use of glue or nails.

Nepalese artists continued Indian traditions in painting and sculpture. Twelfth century Buddhist manuscript illuminations were painted on narrow strips of palm leaf. Each usually contained an individual figure, many resembling first century A.D. Indian sculpture. These oblong illuminations, dictated by the shape of the palm leaf itself, influenced book illustration shapes in Tibet and China long after the material was replaced by silk and paper. Nepalese sculptors made bronze images, modeled upon traditional Indian religious figures.

After Buddhism reached Tibet in the seventh century, the two primary Tibetan art forms were religious images and objects used in rituals. Up to the sixteenth century, the paintings were similar to Indian examples. After this, Chinese painting was also influential.

▲ *This Nepalese stupa design evolved from earlier Indian examples. The square and conical spire and the painted eyes are a Nepalese addition.*

Newar Woodcarving

The Newar people have produced some of the finest woodcarvings in Asia. These architectural decorations have symmetrical, geometric designs or animal configurations. Tools used in the house and field are also richly carved. ∎

Masks carved from wood and ▶ *painted brightly are often used in ritualistic masquerades by the Nepalese and Tibetans. This Tibetan mask depicting Dharmapala, the defender of Buddhist faith, was made between the fourteenth and seventeenth centuries.*

◀ *This richly carved, seventeenth century window frame typifies Newar carving in Nepal. The carved patterns, forming a peacock, transform a flat, exterior brick wall into an ornate work of art.*

▲ *This is the seventeenth century Potala palace of the Dalai Lama on top of one of the highest mountains in Lhasa. Giant* thangkas *can be seen hanging from the walls in front of the palace.*

This sacred ▶
dagger, made of bronze between the sixteenth and seventeenth centuries, would probably have been used in a candlelit Tibetan religious ceremony.

Thangkas

The word *thangka* means something that hangs and is usually a religious scroll painting. Hung above an altar or from the rafters of a house, they were used for meditation purposes. Sometimes they were carried as banners in processions. *Thangkas* first appeared in the tenth century but few survive from before the seventeenth century. ■

Tibetan Buddhist paintings and objects gradually evolved into a unique style. The common form of painting is a *thangka*. These are portraits of historical figures and representations of gods, protectors and mystics. The figures were usually surrounded by the episodes, animals and people associated with them. A finished *thangka* had bright colors and gilt highlights. Different craftspeople were responsible for the different stages of production. The canvas usually had a red and yellow silk border, symbolizing the power centered within, and was sewn onto a larger piece of textile. The painting could be hung from a bamboo rod or rolled up for storage.

Small sacred daggers, thunderbolts, lamps and incense burners made of gold, brass, silver and wood, symbolized elements in Buddhist religious ceremonies. Richly ornamented, everyday objects were finely crafted for nomadic Tibetans. Exquisite silver and leather purses, needlecases, knives and portable boxes to enshrine a Buddha could all be hung from a belt or saddle. They were often decorated with the eight lucky symbols of Tibetan Buddhism. Fine Tibetan carpets, saddle-rugs and temple textiles were also woven.

Nepal and Tibet are two of the economically poorest, yet visually richest, countries in the world. Much Tibetan Buddhist culture was suppressed after Chinese annexation in 1959. Thousands of Tibetans were killed or fled to Nepal or India. The United Nations refugee centers in Nepal oversee the welfare of displaced Tibetans and ensure the continuation of Tibetan arts and culture.

The Dalai Lama

The Dalai Lama (1935–   ) is the head of Tibetan Buddhists and used to rule the country. He lived in the most sacred temple, the Potala, in the capital, Lhasa. When the Chinese invaded Tibet in 1951, the present Dalai Lama was only sixteen. In 1959, the Dalai Lama was forced to flee to India. He is a well known ambassador for Tibetan culture and the most important religious figure for Buddhists everywhere. ■

Tibetans still ▶
consider the Dalai Lama the leader of their country and their religious leader, despite the fact that he was forced to leave Tibet and flee to India in 1959.

7 Neolithic, Bronze Age, Qin and Han Dynasty Art of China

The Three Religions __

There are three important religions in Chinese history. Buddhism became important in China after the third century A.D. Confucianism follows the teachings of the philosopher Confucius (approx. 550–478 B.C.). His writings were based upon the values of traditional Chinese culture. They demonstrate proper conduct and the individual's place in society. Taoism began with the philosopher, Lao Tse (approx. 604–531 B.C.) who spoke of the balancing forces in nature as a means of finding inner tranquillity and harmony with man's surroundings. ■

◀ *This Chinese Neolithic pot was made between 4000 and 3500 B.C. The lower half is left undecorated, probably because it was fixed in sand while the geometric design was painted on the upper portion. It bears some resemblance to the Neolithic pots of ancient civilizations in Greece and Central America. Most earthenware pots are found in tombs. Some are decorated with engraved marks that resemble later Chinese characters.*

The early inhabitants of China made painted pottery in the Neolithic period from about 5000 to about 1700 B.C. Their pots were black or red with some white decoration. Abstract, swirling or geometric designs were painted among animal motifs.

During the Shang Dynasty (1523–1028 B.C.) bronze vessels were made. The range of styles grew more elaborate during the Zhou Dynasty (1027–256 B.C.). Some dated and inscribed vessels were used, for example, in birthday or anniversary ceremonies. Many of the pottery and bronze vessels have been protected in tombs.

This bronze ▶ vessel from about 1500 B.C., was probably used for ritualistic purposes. It would have contained a specific offering of wine, rice or other foods. Most of the vessels have developed a bluish-green patina from contact with the air.

Terracotta Warriors ___

Before 210 B.C., a lavish tomb complex was built by the first emperor. It was discovered outside the modern city of Xian in 1974. The archeological site contains a tomb village of more than 7,500 lifesize clay figures buried row on row. ■

The terracotta warriors from the ▶ tomb complex of the Emperor Qin Shi Huangdi, who died in 210 B.C., are an underground army of soldiers and servants. They represent dutiful warriors, crossbowmen and groomsmen with horses protecting the tomb and the emperor in the afterlife. The figures have a wide range of facial features, elaborate costumes and hair styles. This spectacular archeological find was first discovered in 1974.

◄ Clay models of early Chinese architecture, such as this green-glazed, Han Dynasty watchtower, provide scholars with an idea of the appearance and construction of wooden and tiled structures that have been lost in fires and earthquakes over the centuries. Such a tower would have been used as a watchtower.

Chinese Writing

Chinese writing is more than 6,000 years old and has some 40,000 different characters. Each character is a series of brush-strokes made with a paintbrush and ink, and forms a single-syllable word. Between 2,000 and 5,000 characters have to be memorized before someone can write in Chinese. They are read from top to bottom and right to left. ∎

Ritual vessels were the most important objects in the Bronze Age, from about 1700 to 221 B.C. They were cast in segments and welded together in over one hundred known shapes. Over the centuries, the bronze developed a green patina prized by collectors.

Green, grey, brown or black jade works of art were also made for ceremonial rites. Some were symbolic tools or weapons. Animals, birds, insects or mythical monsters were carved as small three-dimensional pendants for burial in tombs.

The vast Chinese territories were united briefly under the first emperor Qin Shi Huangdi (259–210 B.C.) during the Qin Dynasty (221–207 B.C.). Unification was made possible by the standardization of Chinese script, coins, weights and measures and the establishment of a road network, administrative systems and a code of laws. The first emperor sought to protect his country from invasion by joining up various parts of a wall built in earlier centuries. The Great Wall of China stretched for thousands of miles from what is now Inner Mongolia to the Tibetan border.

The Han Dynasty (206 B.C.–220 A.D.) was a period of great expansion, external trade and technical advance. Death and tomb rituals remained important. Small, glazed ceramic animals in miniature farm enclosures; cooking stoves and vessels; small human figures playing dice, tending ducks, or on horseback with bows and arrows; replicas of wooden houses and watchtowers have all been found. These tomb objects are simply designed and sometimes crudely made, but they are lifelike and reflect a keen awareness of human and animal behavior.

Jade was thought to protect the deceased in the afterlife. When a Han Dynasty emperor or prince died, he was buried in two lacquered coffins, wearing an elaborate suit made of more than 2,000 pieces of jade laced together with gold thread. They were so heavy the outer coffin had to have wheels.

Chinese Symbolism

Decorative elements in Chinese art are laden with symbolism. A bat in Chinese culture is a very good symbol because the word for bat (*fu*) sounds like the word for happiness. The word for fish (*yu*) sounds like the word for abundance or riches. A goldfish pictured on a piece of porcelain suggests an abundance of wealth like all the fish in the sea. ∎

◄ This burial suit made for Queen Tou Wan contains more than 2,000 pieces of jade laced together with gold thread. It dates from the late second century B.C. It would have taken about ten years to make it.

Tang and Song Dynasty Art of China

◀ *Colossal cut stone Buddha figures, like these, demonstrate the importance of the religion soon after its arrival in China. Five such caves were carved at Datong before the capital was moved to Luoyang in 494 A.D.*

Camels and horses ▶ from the Silk Road were included in the tombs during the Tang Dynasty. This earthenware horse and rider has a runny green and mustard yellow glaze.

The Four Treasures___

The four treasures of the Chinese artist are the ink stick, the inkstone, the brush and the paper. The artist takes a small portion of the ink stick, dilutes it with water while grinding it on the inkstone and paints with a bamboo brush on paper or silk. ■

These eighth century earthenware figures of musicians, each playing a different instrument, suggest the vitality of Tang Dynasty women. ▼

The Tang Dynasty (618–906 A.D.) was a period of prosperity and territorial expansion. China's borders reached from Vietnam in the south to beyond the Caspian Sea in the west. Foreign ideas and influences became commonplace in the capital Ch'ang-an. This was a vibrant, well-planned city with tree-lined avenues, canals, gardens and temples.

Buddhism was increasing its hold while Taoism was still practiced. Both religions led to the transformation of architecture and the painted and decorative arts, but Buddhism had the greater influence. Images of the Buddha and his disciples gradually evolved, reshaping many art forms.

The Luoyang area of northern China became the first important site for Buddhist cave shrines. Nearly fifty caves are crowded with wall paintings and early examples of Buddhist inscriptions and monumental statuary, some more than sixty feet/eighteen meters tall. The human figures all have square faces, stiff bodies, patterned drapery and modest ornaments. They were probably modeled on objects and drawings from India.

There was an abundance of smaller sculptural figures and objects for burial in the tombs. Like the Han terracottas, the Tang pieces are realistic but are more graceful, elegant and abundantly detailed. A distinctive combination of mustard yellow, brown and green glazes known as *san-chai*, or three-color, became common for tomb statuary and everyday objects.

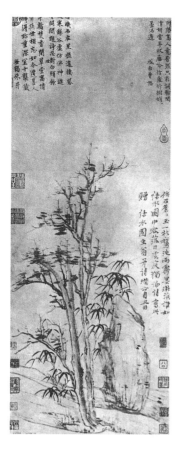

◀ *Ink paintings of bamboo, like this one of the fourteenth century by Ni Tsan, were popular subjects for painters during and after the Yuan Dynasty (1279–1368). Bamboo is a symbol of the scholar-artist because it bends but does not break easily.*

Many beloved glaze colors and patterns began to be produced in the Song Dynasty. This is a celadon wine jug made during that period. ▼

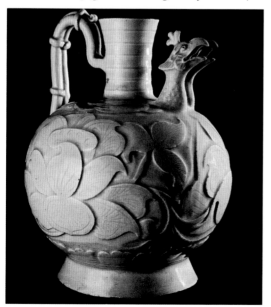

Emperor Hui-Zong

The last important emperor of the northern Song Dynasty (960–1126), Hui-Zong (1082–1135), was a renowned painter and calligrapher. He specialized in painting birds and flowers. As a noted teacher of artists, he set up an official school of painting in the imperial palace. He dictated the styles and subjects for painting that would influence court art for centuries to come. ■

The Tang tomb objects suggest a confident people involved in trade along the Silk Road. The figures include camels ridden by foreigners with dark skins, beards, exotic clothing and jewelry. These outsiders seem to coexist with Chinese people who appear relaxed and secure. The figures of women are active, engaging and seem equal to the men. Women ride horses, play polo and other physically demanding games, and appear confident and in control of their lives.

Short-lived dynasties followed the Tang until the arrival of the Song Dynasty (960–1279). With a return to unity and the reminder of conflicts with barbarians came an awareness of national identity and the importance of native traditions. Manuals for artists were written, encouraging them to strive for technical and aesthetic perfection. Song dynasty painting and porcelain is among the finest ever produced in China.

Painters chose a variety of subjects, including landscape, bamboo, birds and flowers. It was important to portray more than physical appearance. The "soul of nature" had to emerge from the painting, usually rendered in shades of black ink. This spiritual dimension was a direct result of Buddhist or Taoist religious practices.

Ceramics also shifted away from realism and surface ornamentation. The materials and the subtlety of the glazes became critically important. Beauty was in the brevity of line, the lack of decoration and simplicity of form. One-color glazes replaced the earlier three and multi-color glazes. Different kiln sites used either creamy white, bluish-green, brown and white or blue and purple glazes.

Celadon

Celadon is a name for the elegant, blue-green porcelain that began as imperial Song ware. It was copied and modified for centuries. Sometimes the glaze has a network of small cracks and is called a crackle glaze. This was much sought after, but difficult to predict because it depended on the relative expansion and contraction of the clay and the glaze in the kiln. ■

9 Ming Dynasty Art of China

Four Types of Chinese Paintings

A handscroll painting is stored rolled up. It is gradually unrolled for study from right to left, section by section.

A hanging scroll hangs on a wall. Its size and the possibility of viewing it from a distance mean it can be appreciated by a group of people.

A fan painting is a painted image on one or both sides of a fan. Fans were painted by both men and women.

Album paintings were pasted into books. A common format would be a painting on the right-hand page accompanied by a passage of relevant calligraphy on the left. ■

▲ *Chinese lacquer objects, like this Ming box, are usually finished in red or black. Some were particularly prized when encrusted with gold, silver and mother-of-pearl inserts. The pattern of this one is carved.*

A traumatic period in Chinese history followed the Song Dynasty with the arrival of invaders from Mongolia under Genghis Khan. The Mongols set up the Yuan Dynasty (1260–1368) and its great military rulers were generally not patrons of the arts. They laid waste to the land and the population was almost halved, but they allowed Chinese arts and crafts to develop without interference. Many artists began to include more color and greater vitality in their work and less of the spiritual component of Song Dynasty painting. Landscape painting was more realistic.

On the expulsion of the Mongols, one of the longest and most glorious periods began. It is known as the Ming Dynasty (1368–1644). The word "Ming" means brilliant. Artists returned to the work of earlier masters, imitating and refining Tang and Song painting styles. Bold colors, crisp lines and outlines and spirited observations of plants

Lacquerware

Chinese objects made of lacquer date back to about 7000 B.C. Layers of sap from a tree are built up on a textile or wooden base, perhaps in the shape of a bowl or plate, until there is a quarter inch/six millimeter thickness protecting it from water, heat and insects. During the Song Dynasty, lacquer began to be carved. Elaborate pictures, stories or a passage of calligraphy were scratched or incised into the hard surface. ■

◀ *The Chinese artist Hsiao Yün-ts'ung (1596–1673) made this fan painting in 1672 in ink on paper.*

There was a ▶ growing demand in Europe, beginning in the sixteenth century, for blue and white porcelain, such as this Ming vase.

Seals and Chops

A seal is a personal mark made, usually in red ink, with a small tool called a chop. A wood, bronze, stone or horn chop is engraved with Chinese characters identifying its owner. The characters are carved in a special script which has angular, characters of uniform size. ■

The Chinese Garden

A scholar-artist of the Ming Dynasty usually designed a garden adjoining his study. It did not have many colorful flowers but a series of small enclaves of rocks, water and trees symbolizing a lake with islands set among mountains. These miniaturized re-creations of nature provided inspiration for urban artists. ■

◀ *This colorful seventeenth century cloisonné water sprinkler was probably used during a Buddhist ritual. The Chinese learned this method of decorating metal from the Arabs.*

and animals characterized the paintings of Ming Dynasty artists.

The prosperity of the Ming dynasty produced a growing merchant and scholar class with disposable incomes. Houses with elaborate garden complexes were designed in the middle of cities. Furnishings included carved lacquer dishes, cloisonné bowls and exquisite hardwood furniture.

The porcelain market grew dramatically during the Ming Dynasty. The dynamic vigor of the images painted on the pieces greatly increased. Ming vessels became highly colored, elaborately decorated and much grander statements of importance.

After cobalt began to be imported from Persia to make a blue glaze pigment, the city of Jingdezhen became famous for its imperial kilns, which produced blue and white porcelain. Lively designs painted under the glaze included dragons, phoenixes, flowers, animals and fruits, all laden with symbolic meaning. A piece of porcelain would have been studied for its implied message, as one would contemplate a painting to understand the intentions of the artist. This blue and white ware filtered back to Persia where it was copied and made more showy.

Western European traders arriving in China in the sixteenth century were keenly interested in acquiring tea, silk and porcelain. They were particularly fond of the decorative blue and white porcelain which became a staple of the Chinese export trade. It has remained popular throughout the west ever since. It inspired the blue and white delftware made in Holland from the seventeenth century and the blue and white transfer-printed china made in England from the eighteenth century. Chinese style also influenced European furniture and interior and garden design during the eighteenth century.

Cloisonné

Cloisonné is a colorful surface decoration for metal. It reached China from the Arab world along the Silk Road. A pattern is outlined with cloisons, thin metal wires or strips, on a metal base and is filled with powdered enamels of different colors. The object is fired in a kiln. The enamel melts and cools to form a colorful, glassy surface outlined with metal that can be sanded smooth. Some of the finest such work was produced in the fifteenth century for the imperial palace and temples in China. ■

10 Qing Dynasty Art in China

The Art of Manchuria_

Manchuria is the northeastern province of China bordering Russia and North Korea. Manchurian art was influenced by both the Chinese and the Khitans, a nomadic people inhabiting this desolate region. Manchuria was a long way from any major urban area, so their art retains a rustic, provincial appearance, sometimes devoid of sophistication. ■

▲ *The fifteenth century Hall of Supreme Harmony is the most important building in the Forbidden City because it was the site of many important ceremonies.*

The Forbidden City ___

The Forbidden City is the high-walled, imperial complex in Beijing. It included the Hall of Supreme Harmony and the Inner Court, the living quarters of the emperor and empress. Access to the Forbidden City was limited to those of a certain court rank or social status. The complex fell into disrepair after the fall of the imperial system in 1911, but today it is open to the public. ■

◄ *This is a painted corridor from the Empress Cixi's Summer Palace outside Beijing, where the Imperial family stayed during the hot summer months. It contains one of the largest and best preserved Imperial Chinese gardens. The complex, largely rebuilt in the late nineteenth century, includes many pavilions for admiring panoramic views and sunsets over the water.*

By the late sixteenth century, the Ming Dynasty was beginning to disintegrate. There were political and bureaucratic problems and crippling internal rebellions. The Manchus invaded from the north and founded the Qing Dynasty (1644–1911). They were eager to adopt Chinese culture and customs and continued the Chinese system of government. They became keen patrons of the arts.

Not all artists welcomed the arrival of the Manchus. The painter Bada Shanren (1626–1705) was a skilled painter of birds, flowers and rocks. He became disgusted at the Manchus' dominating presence and used his art to protest against their rule. For example, he portrayed lotuses, a symbol of purity, with broken stems. This was a powerful statement about the Qing Dynasty, as the word *qing* means "pure".

The second Qing emperor, Kangxi (1654–1722) who reigned from 1662 until his death, and his grandson, the Qianlong emperor who reigned from 1736 to 1795, were enlightened rulers who courted intellectuals and encouraged scholarship, the fine arts and regional crafts. The Qianlong emperor's reign is often referred to as yet another golden age, as China was becoming one of the wealthiest and most populous countries in the world. He sponsored artists to work in the Forbidden City and assembled a vast art collection of ancient Chinese bronzes.

Much fine porcelain was produced for domestic and export

▲ *This painted hanging scroll,* Bodhidharma Crossing the Yangtze on a Reed, *was painted by the first Qing emperor Shunzhi (1644–61). Shunzhi was more interested in the arts than government. He became an accomplished painter and worked in a freely painted style much admired by Chinese scholars.*

Women Artists in Imperial China __

Although the majority of painters in traditional Chinese society were men, there were also important women artists whose artistic accomplishments were recognized by contemporary male collectors and connoisseurs. Some were the wives or daughters of professional artists learning their craft at home. Others were taught by their mothers, aunts and female tutors. Women painted the same subjects as men, although the majority painted birds, flowers and insects. They were particularly skilled in the textile arts, producing exquisite silk embroidery for clothing and furnishings. ■

markets during the Qing Dynasty, yet most of it imitates the styles of previous centuries. There were few remarkable innovations but there was a tendency to adopt more garish, decadent colors for monochrome glazes. Some of the largest, most ostentatious porcelain was produced during this time. It exemplified the confidence, boastfulness and isolation of eighteenth century China.

A series of humiliating entanglements with western trading countries began in China with the Opium Wars against the British in 1839. Hong Kong and Burma were ceded to the British, while other regions were lost to the Japanese and French-occupied Vietnam. A series of weak emperors and the Sino-Japanese War of 1894 to 1895, coupled with floods, droughts and epidemics at the turn of the century, led to the collapse of the imperial system in 1911. Large, flamboyant pieces of furniture with inlaid mother-of-pearl, multi-colored, carved lacquer dishes and gaudy acid-colored porcelain produced during this period all suggest the decline of society and the country as a whole.

George Chinnery_____

The English artist George Chinnery (1774–1852) spent the last fifty years of his life in Asia, painting views of India before heading to China around 1830. Soon after, he settled in the Portuguese colony of Macao. He produced landscape views and scenes of everyday village life as well as portraits of Asian and European traders of the late Qing Dynasty. He was probably the European artist most successful in capturing the mood of nineteenth century life in colonial Macao and Hong Kong. ■

This finely embroidered silk dragon ▶ *robe, made in the eighteenth century, would have been worn either by the emperor or empress. This was the most common form of palace dress, worn with a belt tied around the waist. It was made from four long tunic panels sewn together. The sleeves have the characteristic imperial horsehoof shaped cuffs. Each robe had nine dragons embroidered in gold thread as nine was a lucky number associated with the emperors.*

11 Twentieth Century Art of China

Mao Zedong

Mao Zedong (1893–1976) was the principal founder of the Chinese Communist party and became the first Chairman of the People's Republic of China in 1949. He sought to create a new society, free of private property and class conflict. He was a calligrapher, poet and writer who outlined Communist doctrine and his beliefs in the *Little Red Book*. Millions of copies were produced. Those who opposed him usually suffered imprisonment or death. ■

Politically related ▶ *crafts, like this Mao button were produced in many styles. Some contained quotations from Chairman Mao.*

The National Palace Museum, Taipei

The Chinese imperial art collection from the Forbidden City, Beijing, was hidden underground hundreds of miles from Beijing to keep it safe from the Japanese. On the Communists' victory, the Nationalists took the collection from the mainland to Taiwan, where they set up their own government. They opened the National Palace Museum in 1965, showing the imperial collection, much to the consternation of the Communist authorities on the mainland who still lay claim to it. ■

▲ *Li Hua (1907–   ) produced this woodcut on paper, entitled* Flood of Wrath, *which shows the Chinese peasants' anger unleashed at their Japanese invaders. He was a leading printmaker of the Modern Woodcut Movement that promoted the use of woodblock prints for portraying the work and struggles of everyday life. This genre, called Social Realism, derived from earlier movements in Germany and Russia.*

After the fall of the Manchu Dynasty, China struggled with the conflict between western and native ideas. The tension between native and foreign styles is best seen in painting. In the late nineteenth century, western influences began to creep in. Popular subjects remained, but bolder and new, more energetic images appeared. Heavy lines, prominent ink splotches and strong colors created more forceful statements about nature and life.

Western teaching methods reached China after 1906, when art schools and studios opened in Peking, Nanking, Shanghai and Hangzhou. After 1920, students flocked to Paris to learn more about Post-Impressionism and Cubism. On their return, they painted in oil instead of ink. A bohemian enclave formed in Shanghai with an untraditional way of life and interests.

Japanese incursions into Manchuria and the 1937 invasion of Peking, presented a dilemma. Bohemian artists advocated "art for art's sake," but the realists yearned for a protesting art of revolt, compatible with Chinese interests.

The Japanese eventually surrendered in 1945, at the end of World War II, but the ensuing civil war battles between Mao Zedong's

The Cultural Revolution

In the late 1950s production in industry and agriculture was failing badly and many people were starving in China. In 1965, to crush his critics, Chairman Mao began a four-year Cultural Revolution. He closed all schools and enlisted millions of teenagers as Red Guards to expose counter-revolutionaries and intellectuals tainted by western thinking. The Red Guards terrorized their elders and destroyed much of China's heritage. Many people were imprisoned and sent to labor camps. Probably, over 10 million people died. The aftermath was felt even after Mao's death in 1976. ■

This model ▶
family eats
under the
watchful eye of
Chairman Mao
during the
Cultural
Revolution.

Communists and Chiang Kai Shek's (1887–1975) Nationalist forces divided China bitterly. Artists' lives changed dramatically after the Communist victory. They were enlisted as agents of the state, working to promote Communist ideals and create a modern socialist state.

Under Mao Zedong's rule, everyone's life was strictly controlled. The unification of the masses was meant to equalize all people. Everyone was required to work for the common interest. Most artists were forced into the fields and factories as manual laborers.

The dreams of internationalism and modernism of the 1920s and 1930s were forgotten. The new art's subjects were drawn from contemporary life: factory productivity, construction work, happy peasants working in fields and the joys of communal living. Only native Chinese methods were allowed. It was against the law to paint with western oils on canvas.

An art genre known as Revolutionary Romanticism depicted the heroism of the worker, boasted of the better life under Communism and proclaimed the superhuman status of the leaders. Chairman Mao was worshipped as a god and his image was omnipresent.

There were a few artists who still managed to produce paintings independent of state control. Chang Dai Chien (1899–1983) experimented with bold painterly brushwork and forceful lines derived from the Abstract Expressionist movement of New York in the 1950s, and yet he produced images that remain inherently Chinese. His large 1968 handscroll, *Ten Thousand Miles of the Yangtze* used traditional media. It is an uneasy painting, portraying the disturbance and dislocation of his crippled country during the Cultural Revolution.

The Communists revived many craft traditions. The Communists created embroidery institutes, hired thousands of jade carvers and mechanized porcelain factories. Carpet patterns were borrowed from eighteenth and nineteenth century France. Exports boomed.

Contemporary Art

China resumed contact with western governments and businesses in 1979. Students were encouraged to produce art independent of government authority. A democracy movement gathered strength, culminating in massive student demonstrations in Tiananmen Square in Beijing where the military forces killed over 1,000 unarmed people June 3–4, 1989. Under Communist rule Chinese artists had to be cautious. Artists' statements could not be too critical of Communist authorities or the artists could be sent to prison. ■

The artist Yuan Yunsheng combines Chinese and western traditions in paintings ▶
such as Drift *of 1980.*

12 Early Art of Japan

The Tale of Genji, ▶ *tells the love stories of the aristocracy of Kyoto, especially those at the emperor's court. Immortalized in Japanese paintings and prints for centuries, the story's elaborate costumes and jewels, rooms divided with sliding doors and gold folding screens and figures fleeing in haste, were well suited to the artist producing episodic narration. This twelfth-century ink and water color on paper handscroll shows a scene from the story.*

The Tale of Genji

The Tale of Genji, the first novel in any language, was written in the late tenth century by Lady Murasaki Shikibu (approx. 978–approx. 1014). Translated into many languages it has become one of the best known Japanese stories in the west. ■

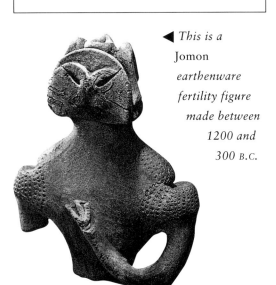

◀ *This is a Jomon earthenware fertility figure made between 1200 and 300 B.C.*

Writing and recorded history reached Japan with the arrival of Chinese civilization in the mid-sixth century A.D. Artifacts discovered from the earlier hunter-gatherer society include much fine pottery called *Joman* pottery, made between 1200 and 300 B.C. Vases with incised and painted abstract patterns were produced for ritual use. The same people also made small mysterious-looking fertility goddesses with large, penetrating eyes shaped like insects or shells.

During the Yagoi period (approx. 300 B.C. to 250 A.D.), Japan evolved into a settled, rice-growing society more typical of east Asia. This allowed for the growth of specialist arts and crafts and for the spread of Shintoism, the Japanese religion based upon spirit worship.

By the mid-sixth century A.D., Japan was a unified country willing to accept both Buddhist and Shinto worship. Buddhism arrived in Japan in 552 A.D. and was adopted by the court. Under imperial

Shintoism

Followers of Shintoism believe in nature spirits, wandering ghosts and spirits of the dead. Its gods, called *kami*, are elements in nature, such as the wind, or concepts, such as the spirit of the country. There is little representation of the Shinto religion in Japanese art, but, because artists incorporate their spirit in the objects they create, the Japanese believe there are Shinto characteristics in all works of art. ■

Nara and Heian

Chinese ideals of government, planning and architecture were imitated when Nara became the capital in 710. The two important temple complexes there were built with monasteries, wall paintings and bronze sculpture.

The Japanese capital moved to Heian in 794. Over the next 300 years, a national art style developed. It was a period of courtly elegance and luxury. Secular, household, art forms prospered. A distinct Japanese painting style, known as *yamato-e*, was developed to depict the opulence and beauty of contemporary life and to illustrate literary tales. ■

▲ *This gold leaf and lacquer Buddha carved in 1053 A.D. by Jocho is one of the finest ever produced in Japan.*

patronage, Buddhism profoundly changed art forms and religious structures. With the arrival of Buddhism came Chinese writing and bureaucracy. The Japanese capital of Nara was established in 710 A.D. and based upon a Chinese design. When the capital was moved to Heian, now Kyoto, at the end of the eighth century, Ch'ang-an, the Chinese capital during the Tang Dynasty was used as a model. Buddhist temples and shrines were erected, beginning one of the most extensive architectural programs in Japanese history.

Japanese sculptures surviving from the early Buddhist period are generally single standing figures or groups of three Buddhas and bodhisattvas. The bronze or gilded-bronze images were used for contemplation by the elite members of society who sought respite from the realities of life. The figures appear stiff and serene, demonstrating the seriousness and austerity of this foreign religion.

Buddhist sculpture after the tenth century was mostly made of wood. Some forms were monumental in scale, richly painted or gilded for added dramatic effect. The most important early Japanese woodcarver was Jocho (approx. 1000–57). His great *Buddha of the Western Paradise* is probably his masterpiece. He appears much softer and more natural than earlier Japanese Buddhas.

There was also a Japanese tradition of large, lacquered, sculptural figures some twelve feet/over three and a half meters tall. These figures had a lighter, more natural, fleshy appearance. Their facial expressions, in particular, took on lifelike qualities.

A form of expressive sculpture, pre-dating the arrival of Buddhism, survived. *Gigaku* wooden masks were used as part of an elaborate,

Zen Buddhism

Buddhism is rich in scriptural texts and artists refer to them to paint images of the Buddha or to carved images of bodhisattvas. An austere sect, Zen Buddhism, was established in the late twelfth century and became widely popular. It was extremely influential in portraiture, austere ink paintings and calligraphy. It was also important for garden design. Rock gardens and configurations of raked sand provided vehicles of contemplation and eventual enlightenment. ■

non-religious temple dance. Their vigorous and barbaric forms descended from the rituals of the nomads of the Siberian steppes. During the ninth century, various styles of dance from Japan, Korea and China were combined to form the *Bugaku* style. The carved and painted masks for the new dance were smaller, more comical and less threatening. The *Bugaku* dance with masks is still the official court dance of Japan.

13 Later Buddhist and Feudal Art of Japan

Shogunate portraits are realistic, yet stylized, images of Japanese rulers. This ink and color on silk handscroll of Minamoto no Yoritomo is attributed to Fujiwara Takanobu (1142–1205). ▼

◀ *Two of the most dramatic wooden sculptures of the Kamakura period were guardian figures for the great south gate of the grand temple of Todai-ji at Nara, made by Unkei in 1203. They were made in sections, allowing the artist greater freedom to twist their bodies, exaggerate their musculature and swirl the drapery.*

A series of civil wars broke out during the twelfth century among the various Japanese warlords. A military government was set up in Kamakura, more than 220 miles/350 kilometers east of the old capital of Heian. Rule by warlords, or shoguns, and their attendant samurai continued until the nineteenth century. The first Kamakura period (1185–1334) was an unsettled time, when swords, armor and military equipment became works of art.

Shogunate portraiture was affected by Zen Buddhist interest in realism and simplicity. The strength and importance of the warlord, Minamoto no Yoritomo, who established the capital at Kamakura, is shown in a commanding hanging scroll of the mid-twelfth century. The artist Fujiwara Takanobu (1142–1205) probably gives the viewer an accurate account of the shogun's cold, commanding appearance.

During the Kamakura period, real-life settings and dramas became suitable subjects for *yamato-e* narrative handscrolls. The civil wars among the warlords were now portrayed as terror-filled conflicts or

World of Shoguns and Samurai

A shogun was a military leader. Shoguns were the highest ranking officials in Japan right up to 1868. They assumed importance after the civil wars ended in the late twelfth century and exercised political power as well as military might. A shogun's soldiers were the samurai. During the shogunate period, this warrior class in society overtook the aristocratic class in wealth and prosperity. ■

The warriors known as samurai wore elaborate suits of armor, ▲
such as this one made in 1859 in steel, iron and leather.

▲ *Portrayals of hell are a well established genre in Japanese painting. In this detail from a hanging scroll, of about 1200, called* Jigoku Zoshi, *horse-headed demons strike at monks and chase them through the gates of hell.*

Kimonos

A kimono is a floor-length, long-sleeved silk gown worn by Japanese women. A large band called an *obi* was tied around the waist, usually of a complementary color or contrasting pattern. Kimonos are still worn in Japan today, but usually for ceremonies and special occasions. ■

Masks like this one were used in a No *drama of the eighteenth century.* ▼

The Art of the Sword _____

Under shogunate rule, swords were very important and their creation was almost a religious rite. The famous sword-making schools, formed between the twelfth and fourteenth centuries, passed the mysteries of their craft, only to their families. There were swords for battle and swords for ceremonial purposes. The blades were of varying lengths. Many were signed and dated by the swordsmith. Scabbards evolved into elaborate decorative objects with silver and gold, inlaid designs. ■

bloody tales of heroic warriors, using strong colors, caricature and dramatic actions. All these components are evident in eleventh and twelfth century graphic depictions of the horrors of the eight layers of the Japanese Buddhist hell. Another fourteenth century tradition involved refined performances of dance and drama. These were called *No* dramas, derived from earlier dances of the Heian period. Unlike their *Gigaku* and *Bugaku* predecessors, *No* performances included dialogue extolling the virtues of folk heroes and legendary figures.

During the Muromachi period (1392–1573) interest in Zen Buddhism reached new heights. The religion appealed to aristocrats, priests, scholars and the samurai. Everyone was encouraged to become more Buddha-like. Through introspection, one could embark upon the best course of action in life. The samurai studied meditation which sharpened the powers required for martial arts.

Interest in Zen ink painting and calligraphy was never greater than at this time. Contemplation and monastic discipline were aided by the study of ink paintings. The pictorial images and calligraphic characters are renowned for an economy of ink and brevity of line.

The Japanese tea ceremony has its origins in this period. It involves simple, rustic-looking ceramics and metal tea kettles. The art of preparing, serving and enjoying tea has evolved over the centuries into a ritual and a special room is reserved for it in Japanese houses.

The Folding Screen _____

A Japanese folding screen usually had six hinged panels painted with one continuous narrative. The composition flows uninterrupted over the seams of the panels. There were eight components for a landscape, called "The Eight Views," including a fishing village, an autumn moon, a storm in the mountains and geese descending upon a sandbar. The artist would portray them all somewhere in the composition. ■

14 Japanese Secular Art

▲ *This is an Imari porcelain decanter made in the seventeenth century.*

The Japanese Garden

Chinese garden art inspired the Japanese garden. Early Japanese gardens contained ponds studded with large rocks, symbolizing islands. During the fifteenth century, Zen gardens were popular. A walled enclosure surrounded these gardens. White pebbles, raked in parallel lines, simulated water and boulders symbolized mountains. ■

▲ *A Zen garden or "dry landscape" was appreciated and contemplated from a slightly raised platform. This modest Zen garden in Kyoto, was constructed in the 1480s.*

Domestic turmoil continued into the sixteenth and seventeenth centuries in Japan. During the Momoyama period (1573–1615) shoguns built castles to protect their territories. Momoyama was the name of a castle belonging to a great general, Toyotomi Hideyoshi (1536–98), who unified Japan, made important reforms and began foreign contact. It was a rich period for the arts. The shoguns made unsuccessful invasions of Korea and sent two missions to Europe. For a

Imari Porcelain

Brightly colored Imari ware was designed for export. It appealed to the eighteenth century European fashion for oriental objects. Some pieces portray Portuguese and Dutch sailors with their ships, the details all derived from hearsay. Imari porcelain influenced European design. ■

while there were Dutch, Portuguese and English trading missions in Japan. European Christian missionaries followed and their influence was felt in political circles. It began to be feared that the Christians were intending to conquer Japan. In 1587 Christianity was banned and seven Jesuits were executed in 1597. By 1614 all European Christian missionaries had been expelled and Japan resumed its seclusion from the rest of the world.

Japanese contact with the west inspired an art form called *namban*, "southern barbarian arts." Early seventeenth century paintings, screens and decorative objects show curiosity about the west. Curly-haired, inquisitive Europeans in court attire stand before naive and dreamlike landscapes.

Castle interiors of the Monoyama were very dark and had small windows. Lavishly painted, gilt screens helped reflect what light there was. Gilded sliding doors, murals and ceiling paintings visually united the opulent rooms. The magnificent screens demonstrate the showy, boastful nature of the Monoyama period.

In 1598, the Japanese brought pottery as well as potters back when they retreated from Korea, influencing Japanese work profoundly. Some of the most imaginative designs in Japanese ceramics appeared during the seventeenth and eighteenth centuries, including Imari ware, usually glazed in strong primary colors. Tea drinking also boosted ceramic design. Around 1574, the potter Chojiro (1516–92) invented raku tea bowls. Their irregular shape and rough texture

▲ *Katsushika Hokusai (1760–1849) established landscape as a new important print genre. This famous image is called* Fuji in Clear Weather, *in English, but* Red Fuji, *in Japanese. It portrays the famous conical mountain on Honshu Island in central Japan. Produced about 1830, it is part of a series of thirty-six views of the famous mountain. Hokusai was also well known for his humorous cartoons.*

Hokusai and Hiroshige

Two of the popular Japanese nineteenth century woodblock print artists were Katsushika Hokusai and Ando Hiroshige (1797–1858). Hokusai was famous for his humorous cartoons and sketches, as well as portrayals of the Japanese landscape.

Hokusai's work inspired Hiroshige to produce two important series of travel prints of the Japanese countryside. His lyrical and anecdotal portrayal of common people during the mid-nineteenth century were admired by western print collectors throughout the twentieth century. ■

complemented the asymmetry of the specially decorated tearooms.

The Tokugawa Shogunate followed Hideyoshi's death. Edo, now Tokyo, became the capital in 1603. Edo, Kyoto and Osaka soon began to grow. Isolation, military rule and feudalism continued for 200 years, during this time known as the Edo period.

The screen painting tradition continued through the seventeenth century. A style of screen evolved for the newly emerging, wealthy, merchant class. Townspeople at work, at play or at festivals were now portrayed. There was wider sponsorship of artists producing smaller decorative objects. Miniature carvings, metalwork, lacquer and prints were plentiful and appealed to the masses during the Edo period.

Kabuki theater, based on Japanese historical tales, became popular with city people. This led to an interest in colorful, highly ornate, western-influenced, woodblock prints of famous actors and actresses. Another type of Japanese print, *ukiyo-e*, the art of the everyday, or the passing world, became popular. All sorts of people are seen in these prints.

Japan's isolation began to relax during the 1840s. The shoguns could no longer stop the eager western traders. In 1853, American battleships reached Japan. Two Japanese ports were opened for trade and diplomatic relations with western powers followed. Turmoil among the Japanese led to civil war as the country came to grips with the outside world.

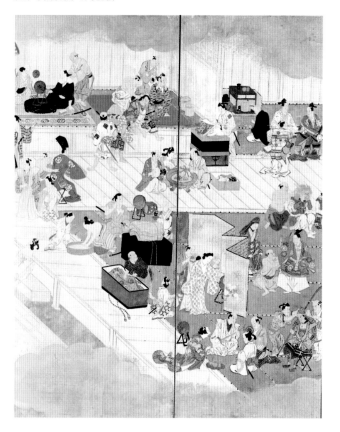

This detail from a seventeenth century screen ▶ *painting attributed to Hishikawa Moronobu shows the behind-the-scenes preparation in a* kabuki *theater. The painting shows the great number of people involved in staging a* kabuki *performance.*

15 Meiji Period and Modern Art of Japan

我驅逐艦隊於旅順港外近接
敵艦激戰大破敵隊

▲ *This print, attributed to Tsukioka Kogyo, depicts a Japanese naval destroyer encountering a Russian battleship off Port Arthur in Manchuria on April 13, 1904. The portrayal of Japanese military might was rendered in strong colors for newspaper readers eager to learn the events of the war.*

Russo-Japanese War Prints

Printmakers were important in conveying the new nationalism and the glorification of the Japanese Empire in the early years of the twentieth century. Their work advertised the heroics of the Japanese military against the Chinese and the Russians. Multi-colored woodblock prints of Russo-Japanese battles in 1904 and 1905 were sold in Tokyo within a week of the particular event. ■

The emperors of Japan had been powerless under the shoguns, but in 1867, the emperor established a western style, provisional government and moved his court from Kyoto to the capital Edo, renamed Tokyo. Feudalism and samurai power were abolished. The Meiji restoration period lasted until 1912. European books were translated, western-style science and literature schools were built and modernization gathered pace.

Under such sweeping influence, western methods became widespread. Mediocre paintings in oil were produced by Japanese artists. To reinvigorate the faltering native art, the Japan Art Academy was founded in Tokyo in 1898. Leading painters combined Japanese and western art methods to revitalize a nineteenth century art movement called *Nihonga*. The artists' use of color, simple lines, decorative detail and atmospheric brushwork suggests an updated, native Japanese art style.

Japanese art forms captured the attention of western artists. Traditional Asian styles were important in the designs of the American architect, Frank Lloyd Wright (1869–1959). He worked in Tokyo between 1915 and 1922 and designed the famous Imperial Hotel in Tokyo to be earthquake proof. It withstood the quake that leveled Tokyo in 1923. On his return to the United States, Wright integrated Japanese design elements and Zen-inspired simplicity in his work. For

▲ *This late nineteenth century oil on canvas is entitled* Garden in Spring *by Asai Chu (1856–1906). The choice of subject matter, composition, brushwork and treatment of light suggests the influence of the French painter Jean-Baptiste-Camille Corot (1796–1875) and the French Impressionists.*

Tadanori Yokoo (1936–) has produced works, like many other post-World War II, Japanese artists, about the atomic bombs that were dropped on the cities of Hiroshima and Nagasaki. He silkscreened this image on ceramic tiles, entitled Postwar (The Direct Aftermath of World War II) *in 1986. Yokoo, a graphic artist living in Tokyo, combines a western Pop Art style with the Japanese ukiyo-e style. He also is a designer of theater sets.* ▼

example, he used large windows looking out over gardens and green spaces to unite people's living quarters and nature.

With so much change, there was much disruption in Japanese society after 1912. A new national identity and sense of purpose were needed and a determination arose to claim more territory. This was seen as a legitimate means of maintaining national and imperial prestige as well as increasing access to raw materials and markets. There were incursions into Manchuria and China in the late 1930s. The Japanese occupied much of east Asia during World War II (1939–45) but eventually surrendered to the Allies, who had dropped atomic bombs on Hiroshima and Nagasaki. This wartime use of nuclear weapons was devastating and traumatizing beyond all experience and many artist-survivors responded to this horror.

Western aid helped rebuild Japan after World War II. During the 1950s and 1960s, industry and commerce were reinvigorated and exports boomed. This fueled the Japanese economy, leading to the prosperity of the 1980s. Many private and corporate art collectors emerged. Private museums and galleries opened in Tokyo, some specializing in Japanese art, others in western art. The Japanese art market became so powerful that it could determine art prices.

Contemporary Japanese art has influenced the west: the sleek lines and minimalist appearance of cars, furniture, glassware, electrical appliances and graphics derive from Zen principles. Western graphic artists in the 1960s and 1970s were captivated by contemporary Japanese prints. The dynamic angles, bold juxtaposition of black and red ink and the blank, undecorated areas within posters, billboards and advertisements point directly to Japanese influence.

The Japanese government promotes contemporary crafts. The title "Living National Treasure" is bestowed on the greatest craftspeople who preserve and pass on traditional techniques.

Contemporary Art in Japan

Many contemporary Japanese art issues resemble those in the west. Sometimes the museum public is unwilling to recognize the artistic merits or serious intentions of a creative artist. Censorship is of great concern. Nobuyuki Ohura (1949–) produced a series of fourteen prints entitled, *Holding Perspective (1982–1985)*, including unflattering depictions of the late Japanese Emperor Hirohito (1901–89). The prints received hostile criticism. The Toyama Prefectural Museum of Modern Art sold the offending prints and burned 470 copies of the catalog produced to show them. ■

16 Art of Korea

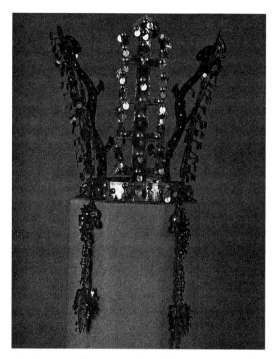

▲ *Ornate gold crowns dating between 400 and 700, were excavated from the royal tombs of the Early and Unified Silla periods.*

This bronze, ▶ *seventh century, meditative religious figure, is called the* Maitreya. *The figure was a popular bodhisattva during the Unified Silla period. His elegant pose suggests an untroubled state of contentment while he quietly contemplates earthly concerns.*

Chinese culture was the first to influence the Korean peninsula. Early Korean hunter-gatherers ventured into China and brought back stone tools and pottery. Towards the middle of the fourth century B.C., iron arrived in northern Korea from China. Intermittent centuries of struggle followed and sometimes the Japanese controlled parts of the country.

Tang culture and bureaucracy left the greatest Chinese legacy during the Unified Silla period (668–935 A.D.). The capital, Kyongju, became a cosmopolitan center where Buddhism became the state religion, inspiring artists, craftsmen and architects. Chinese script also began to be used in the capital.

The Koreans explored Buddhism as their own religion. Sixth to eighth century sculptures, particularly in bronze and stone, are simplified, sometimes abstracted forms, suggesting the grace, dignity and spirituality of Buddhism.

Korean Jewelry of the Unified Silla Period

Korean jewelry of the Unified Silla period was the most accomplished and dramatically beautiful in east Asia. Exquisite work was produced in gold, silver and semi-precious stones. Elaborate crowns excavated from royal tombs were decorated with abstract flowers, tree branches on fire or antlers. Necklaces had comma-shaped beads made of colored glass, jade or quartz. They may have been meant to look like animal fangs or claws. ■

The Mongols overran Korea in 1259. This inspired the Koreans to consider their national identity. Confucianism and Buddhism coexisted peacefully during this period. Confucianism provided the order in society while Buddhism provided the anchor of spiritual peace. Artists and craftspeople produced important porcelain and paintings in innovative native styles. Ceramic production was particularly significant, with Korean celadon rivaling contemporary Chinese pieces in beauty and craftsmanship.

During the Koryo period (935–1392), Korean books were printed by woodblock. A set of 81,137 woodblocks, completed in 1251, forms the world's oldest set of Buddhist scriptures. Korean craftsmen invented movable metallic metal type in 1234.

A Korean alphabet was designed in 1446 at the behest of the scholarly

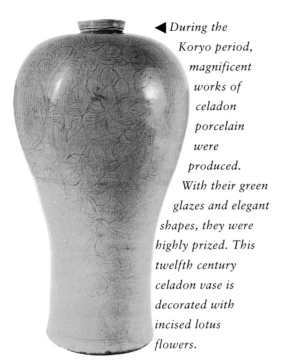

◄ During the Koryo period, magnificent works of celadon porcelain were produced. With their green glazes and elegant shapes, they were highly prized. This twelfth century celadon vase is decorated with incised lotus flowers.

Korean Celadon _____

The best period for Korean porcelain was the eleventh and twelfth centuries. Celadon evolved in Korea at the same time as it evolved in China, but in a different way. Some shapes resemble Chinese work, but many others were shaped like the lotus, the holy flower of Buddhism. The Koreans preferred soft, gray-toned blue-green glazes and more ornate decoration. Before 1150, most celadon was decorated with incised, stamped or molded motifs. Later, more complex inlaid or underglaze decoration, with white, gray and black pictorial patterns of cranes and bamboo or ducks and reeds were common. ■

Korean landscape styles are indebted to the ► Chinese landscape tradition. They contain many make-believe mountains and dramatic vistas for contemplation. This eighteenth century ink and watercolor work on paper entitled Boating Party *by Sin Yun Bok incorporates such an imaginary landscape as a backdrop for this charming scene.*

King Sejong who reigned from 1418 to 1450. Previously, all Korean writing had used Chinese characters. Now, a simpler, phonetic system of twenty-eight signs was invented. The system is still used today.

The Japanese navy invaded Korea in 1592, and destroyed farms, villages and pottery kilns. They returned home with many Korean craftsmen and potters who influenced arts and crafts designs in Japan in the following centuries.

From the eighteenth century the Japanese exerted their cultural influence on Korea. This culminated in Japan's annexation of Korea in 1910. During the next thirty-five years, the Japanese outlawed the use of the Korean language and required Koreans to speak Japanese. Korea was freed from Japanese control at the end of World War II, but following a civil war between 1950 and 1953, Korea was partitioned.

The North Korean Communist regime does not allow artistic creativity or self-expression. There is little room for art or craft forms in daily living. The economic poverty of the country is mirrored by its artistic poverty.

South Korea has a pro-western form of government. It is prosperous and rich in culture with many art galleries and museums. The National Museum of Contemporary Art opened in the capital, Seoul, in 1995. South Korean artists explore the latest trends and developments of other leading art capitals and produce innovative work in many different forms.

Many craftspeople continue to produce work similar to that of earlier centuries. High-quality, handmade paper is an art form practiced today with a history that goes back to the first century A.D.

17 Art of Burma and Thailand

Burma, now called Myanmar, was settled by two Buddhist peoples: the Pyu and the Mon. Their art resembles Buddhist sculpture of the Indian Gupta period. In 1044, the Myanmar invaded and set up their capital, Pagan, on the Irrawaddy River. A golden age for art lasted until the Mongol conquest.

The ruins of Pagan are an architectural wonder. Although the wooden palaces have disappeared, the surviving stupas and temples are commanding symbols of Pagan's power and glory. Stupas at Pagan were based on earlier Pyu and Mon designs. A bell-shaped structure stood on an octagonal base on a terrace, and tapered into a narrow cone.

Many Pagan temples were rich with frescoes similar to sixth century Indian frescoes at Ajanta. This tradition may have been passed down from Pyu and Mon painters. Pagan designs and images also suggest contact with Ceylon, now called Sri Lanka.

Burmese art never recovered from the overthrow of Pagan. Burma languished under the shadow of India and China, until, in 1826, Great Britain made it an extension of its empire. Burma was fought over during World War II and in 1948 it left the British Commonwealth to become an independent republic. The present Burmese military dictatorship limits foreign contact, though a growing

◀ This large, white, brick and stucco temple was built in about 1105 by King Kyanzittha who reigned from 1084 to 1113. It is the most famous of the Pagan temples. It is a memorial to the life and legend of the Buddha and once held 1,400 stone panels illustrating the final days of the Buddha. Glazed tiles, relief carvings and sculptural figures relate episodes of the Buddhist doctrine.

Lacquerware

The art of making lacquer spread to Burma from China. Burmese lacquerware is usually dark orange or black, sometimes with mustard yellow or green highlights. The layers of resin make a smooth, durable surface on which designs can be etched. ∎

This Burmese stele of the ▶ twelfth to thirteenth century is carved with scenes from the life of Buddha. A stele is an upright piece of stone carved with an image, such as this one, or an inscription. Each of the tiny figures that surrounds the large Buddha, leans forward slightly with eyes cast downward. This helps balance the busy composition and creates focus on the central figure of Buddha who reaches down to touch the earth.

▲ *In the nineteenth century, a wealthy person in Thailand would have owned highly prized betel holders like these made of silver, arranged on a silver tray.*

Betel Chewing

People in southeast Asia commonly chew betel leaves and nuts. They are chewed and spat out. Small craft and art objects are produced for the ritual and include storage containers, tools and small boxes made of bamboo, woven reeds, lacquer, brass, silver and sometimes gold. ■

◀ *This early sixteenth century guardian figure was carved in wood for the door of a temple in Thailand in the Ayutthaya school style.*

democracy movement is led by the Nobel Peace Prize winner, Aung San Suu Kyi (1945–). Burmese lacquerware, silver and textiles have a long tradition and are prized by collectors.

Early Thai art reflected a diversity of religious and cultural influences. Buddhism reached Thailand from the Mon in Burma. The Buddhist Dvaravati school flourished from the sixth to the eleventh centuries, making stone, bronze and stucco Buddhas. The Srivijaya School of the eighth to the thirteenth centuries arose from a culture that spread up the Malay peninsula from Sumatra in Indonesia. Srivijayan sculpture shows direct inspiration from Indonesian Buddhas.

The most significant style, Lopburi art, was inspired by the visually rich and powerful Khmer culture centered around Angkor Wat, the principal group of Khmer temples in neighboring Cambodia. Khmer-influenced art appeared in Thailand from the seventh century and

◀ *This Thai silk and cotton shawl, made about 1950, includes repeating geometric designs made of brightly-colored silk threads. It was worn for ceremonial purposes.*

came into its own in the twelfth and thirteenth centuries. It combined aspects of Buddhism and Hinduism, with masculine, square jawed Buddhas, with prominently marked lips and eyebrows.

In the second half of the thirteenth century a native Thai style evolved in three schools. The Sukhothai School, named after the kingdom of Sukhothai in central Thailand, which flourished between the late thirteenth and the fifteenth centuries, was both prolific and influential. Bronze Buddha images portray an idealized, graceful and spiritual Buddha, less masculine than the Lopburi-Khmer style.

The Ayutthaya school came from the kingdom of Ayutthaya, founded in 1350. This was a glorious, unified period when Thailand exerted its influence over the Malay peninsula. The art is a synthesis of traditions throughout the country.

The Bangkok School also grew out of earlier traditions, but the nineteenth century brought renewed interest in mural painting. Western perspective inspired Thai artists to paint in a more naturalistic way. The Bangkok school continues to exert its influence today.

18 Art of Cambodia, Vietnam, Laos, Malaysia and Singapore

The Angkor Period

The Angkor period, from the early ninth century to the early fifteenth century, is when the Khmer kings ruled from a series of magnificent architectural complexes in central Cambodia. King Jayavarman II, who reigned from 802 to 850 established the capital at Roluos and created a state religion. Another important king, Suryavarman II, ruled between 1131 and 1150. He built Angkor Wat, the most important Khmer temple complex. By the twelfth century, Khmer culture controlled mainland southeast Asia and its sculpture and architectural decoration were produced throughout the region. ■

▲ *Angkor Wat is one of the architectural wonders of the world. The elaborate complex of sculptured galleries, temples and vast courtyards is surrounded by a moat.*

Between the ninth and fifteenth centuries, Cambodian Khmer art was influenced by Hinduism from India, Buddhism from Indonesia and the Champa kingdoms in neighboring Vietnam. Eventually, Khmer art developed into a distinct style with three art forms:

▲ *This is a twelfth to thirteenth century portrait in stone of* Jayavarman VII, *who built the Bayon temples. The gentle smile is typical of Khmer-style carvings.*

▲ *The thirteenth century Angkor period temple carvings depict soldiers in battle, fishermen, dancers, musicians and even palm readers. They present a complete record of Cambodian life in the thirteenth century. This particular carving shows a cock-fight.*

▲ *These ornate bronze Dongson drums were made in about 500 B.C. They were probably symbols of power and prestige although their precise use is unknown.*

This mid-ninth century sandstone head of the Hindu god, Shiva, is of the Champa culture in Vietnam. Originally, the work would have been attached to a simply carved body but this has not survived. The facial expression suggests fear and terror. The carved, worm-like halo is characteristic of Cham art. ▼

The Dongson Drums

The huge bronze kettle drums of the Dongson culture are the earliest works of art discovered in southeast Asia. The squat drums are elaborately decorated. Some have small bronze frogs or ritualistic dancers on their rims. The drums have been found throughout southeast Asia, proving there were trading links between northern Vietnam and other parts of the region. The decorative details suggest the influence of the Chinese bronze culture of the Shang and Zhou periods of about 1000 B.C. ■

temples, temple carvings in relief and sculpture.

Khmer temples were made of brick or sandstone and surrounded by water. They represented Mount Meru, the home of the Hindu gods. In the center was an image of the god-king and images of other gods were placed in surrounding towers.

Angkor Wat is a square complex built in the twelfth century as a temple-mausoleum. Dominating the complex is a central pyramid and five towers, balanced with cloisters and galleries. The corridors of the inner courtyards are filled with relief carvings of the characters from Hindu epics. A nearby Buddhist temple complex, Bayon, of a similar design, was built in the late twelfth or early thirteenth century.

The stronger culture of Vietnam and Thailand overwhelmed the Angkor style in the fifteenth century. Like Laos and Vietnam, Cambodia became a French protectorate in 1863. A series of civil conflicts crippled the country before and after the rise of the regime of Pol Pot (1925–   ) in 1975. Pol Pot was responsible for the deaths of two million Cambodians or thirty percent of the population. Much Cambodian architecture was destroyed and nearly all the country's art historians and archeologists were killed. Since 1992, with United Nations peacekeeping forces in place, the Angkor Wat complex and surrounding temples are slowly being restored and reopened.

The Dongson culture in Vietnam existed between 500 and 200 B.C., centered on the Gulf of Tonkin coast of northern Vietnam. The people had contact with the Chinese to the north and traded with islands as far south as southern Indonesia. Their finest art forms were magnificent bronze drums.

The second period of Vietnamese culture is the Champa (second century A.D.–1720). The kingdom of Champa was along the coastal areas near Danang. Seventh century Cham art was influenced by Hindu Gupta art. By the ninth century, Cham art had developed a distinct style. In the tenth and eleventh centuries, sculpture showed Khmer influence. Faces became more human, bodies more graceful and flowing. Champa was overrun by its neighbors in 1471 and was

▲ *With the civil war and its aftermath behind him, the Vietnamese artist Viet Dung (1962–) paints simple, lyrical images of tranquility and prosperity. This is* Girl with Bird, *painted in oil on canvas in 1996.*

Laotian Textiles

Women of all ages weave textiles in Laos. Weaving demonstrates a young woman's potential as a future wife. Much fine cloth is still produced in the Luang Prabang region of central Laos. This was the capital of the kingdom between the fourteenth and nineteenth centuries, and here the finest weavers were employed under court patronage. Decorative *ikat* weavings, a fine type of tie-dyed textile, are produced in central and southern Laos. Those of southern Laos are influenced by Cambodian designs. ■

This cotton and silk textile was made in ▶ *Laos in the mid-1930s. Different ethnic groups in Laos produce distinctive textiles. Nearly all include striped or geometric patterns in strong colors. Some have animal designs or small patterns, like these deer and geometric flowers.*

Laotian Buddhas

Buddhas in Laos have developed differently from elsewhere in Asia. The nose is shaped like an eagle's beak, the earlobes are flat and elongated like long earrings and the hair has tight curls. Buddha often stands with hands pointing towards the ground, and arms held straight down a short distance from the body, calling for rain. Another Laotian pose where the Buddha stands with his hands crossed in front of his body is called "Contemplating the Tree of Enlightenment." ■

greatly reduced in later centuries. In 1720, the king and his remaining people fled to Cambodia to escape their Vietnamese neighbors.

The people of Vietnam lived for centuries under the shadow of the Chinese. Then the French arrived. Initially, the French wanted to end persecution of their Christian missionaries. Then, to control the region's trade routes, they overthrew the Vietnamese emperor in 1862.

Vietnamese nationalism rose during the twentieth century. By 1954, the French had been driven out and the country divided. Civil war broke out. American and Australian forces, backing the South Vietnamese, attempted to stop the advance of Communist North Vietnam. After immense destruction and loss of life South Vietnam surrendered in April 1975. Foreign contact was forbidden, many artists were imprisoned and what artistic expression remained became highly politicized until the late 1980s, when tensions began to calm.

Twentieth century Vietnamese art mirrors historical events. In the 1920s and 1930s, Vietnamese artists were inspired by art movements in Paris. Between 1945 and 1975, artists produced harrowing images of their country at war. With the reopening of Vietnam to the west, there has been a dramatic revival in contemporary painting and

▲ *Many artists in Malaysia today study art in western countries. Sharifa Fatimah Zubir (1948–), who painted* Solitude *in acrylic on canvas in 1989, studied in Great Britain and the United States.*

Malaysian *Songket*

The cloth of gold called *songket* is produced in Malaysia and Indonesia for ornate sarongs, headcloths and scarves. Many weavers work together to produce one length of cloth. Traditionally, the cloth was handwoven silk with gold or silver threads. *Songket* was made for royalty and the designs included ornamental Islamic flowers, geometric patterns or portions of Arabic calligraphy. Its use has spread through society as today less costly materials are used. ■

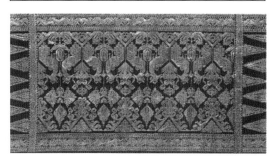

▲ *This beautiful silk and gold* songket *cloth would have been worn for ceremonial purposes.*

sculpture. The lyrical forms and colors of French art have returned.

The range of art styles in mountainous and impoverished Laos was never as great as in neighboring Thailand. Decorative carvings, sculpture and textiles are the major Laotian art forms. Scenes from the Indian epic, the *Ramayana*, are carved on door and window frames. The best sculpture from Laos was produced between the sixteenth and eighteenth centuries. Laotian Buddhas are quite different and have special poses. Colorful, contemporary Laotian textiles have a wide range of styles, sometimes unique to a particular village.

For centuries, small arts and crafts objects have been the major focus of art in Malaysia. One important district is in the center of the Malaysian peninsula and the other is in east Malaysia in Sarawak, part of the island of Borneo.

Basket weaving is very widespread and uses many materials, including bamboo, palm leaves, reeds and rattan. Kite-making is a highly developed craft. The most famous kite design is the huge, crescent-shaped *wau bulan* or moon kite. Kites may also resemble leaves, cats or other animal shapes.

Carved wooden objects decorate doorways, railings, and shutters on public buildings. Because Malaysia is a Muslim country, only floral and animal motifs are allowed.

The skill of making batik tie-dyed textiles reached Malaysia in the seventeenth century from Indonesia. The richly patterned cotton is very colorful and usually printed in long lengths. It is used for all forms of clothing.

Fine silver and pewter work is produced. Intricate designs for silver brooches, belts and rings combine traditional and contemporary motifs. A favorite is the hibiscus, the national flower of Malaysia. Fine vases, water jugs, and trays are made in pewter, often showing the evenly marked surface of metal beaten into shape with a hammer.

Another important craft is bamboo carving. Intricate geometric patterns, scratched into the surface, are stained with dye. The colored dye gets trapped in the carving, and makes the design stand out.

Singapore is most widely known as an extemely prosperous city-state. Lee Kwan Yew's (1923–) strict rule since independence in 1959 determined social and political policies for decades. It produced a society with little room for individual creativity. Although he left office in 1990, his views still affect artists. Contemporary paintings and prints criticizing the government or society may be confiscated, and the artist sued for defamation. Controversial art is not allowed. There is a brisk art market, but the contemporary art on display appears conservative and lacks the challenging edge of much recent art in the west. Popular subjects include Chinese brush paintings, flower pictures and abstract landscapes.

19 Art of Australia and New Zealand

The Aborigines

The Aborigines were the original nomadic inhabitants of Australia and Tasmania, who came from southern Asia some 40,000 years ago. There were 300,000 of them in 1788, but 50,000 in 1888. Today, they again number around 300,000 or 1.7 percent of the population. In the 1930s the Australian government created Aboriginal reservations in central and northern Australia. In the past twenty years, there has been a growing movement seeking rights and staking claims to lands lost to European immigrants. Some Aborigines have integrated successfully into white Australian society. ■

▲ *Rock paintings, such as these painted using pigment on rock, unite modern day Aborigines with their ancestors, who also made paintings like these as long ago as 20,000 years.*

▲ *This Aboriginal artist works carefully to apply dyes to a piece of bark to create a painting of a tribal dance.*

The oldest surviving Aboriginal art forms are stone engravings dating back 20,000 years. They portray skeleton-like birds, animals and spirit people. Stone engravings and cave paintings were created for many centuries. Where there were forests, tree bark was charred over a slow fire and artists incised designs on the sooty surface. Later, geometric and animal designs were painted on the bark in brown, yellow and cream.

Aboriginal art was associated with the phenomenon of dreamtime. This is a trance-like state uniting contemporary Aborigines with their ancestors who emerged from the night to create the world and whose spirits entered all things. Aboriginal rituals recreate the powerful legends of dreamtime. The images of the spirits in stone engravings and bark paintings transmitted stories down the generations as the Aborigines had no written language. Aborigines also paint their bodies for ritual dances, decorate sacred stones, weapons and utensils and carve tree trunks.

▲ *These Aborigines, photographed in the nineteenth century, painted their bodies and wear tribal ceremonial dress. In the foreground is a totem pole carved from a tree trunk.*

For the first hundred years of colonial settlement, Europeans dismissed Aboriginal art as meaningless and barbaric. In the 1880s missionaries and museum curators became interested in this art and began to collect it. In the twentieth century, modern artists began to seek inspiration from primitive art. The encroachment of western art and culture upon Aboriginal communities has been devastating. The original meaning and use of their art forms was gradually lost to the Aborigines. However, many organizations have been set up to address the problem. Aboriginal culture is now sometimes used to represent the national Australian identity.

The first British colony in Australia was established in 1788. The newcomers felt their surroundings to be a lush, romantic Garden of Eden. Many of the wealthier settlers tried to tame the wilderness and artists such as Joseph Lycett (1774–1825), captured their pride in the discovery of a new world in their paintings.

▲ *Sidney Noland (1917–1992) is probably Australia's best known modern artist internationally. Nolan painted this view of the Australian landscape entitled* Musgrave Ranges *in oil on board in 1949.*

Heidelberg School

The Australian painter Tom Roberts led an art colony based in Heidelberg, in Victoria, between 1885 and 1901. Among its members were Charles Condor, Frederick McCubbin and Arthur Streeton. The group camped in a remote area outside Melbourne and painted in the French Impressionist style. They often painted on wooden cigar box lids, so their first, public exhibition in 1889 was called the *9 x 5 Impression Exhibition.* ∎

◀ *An artist of the Heidelberg School, Arthur Streeton painted* The Purple Noon's Transparent Might *in oil on canvas in 1896.*

Contemporary Art in Australia

There are active artists' communities in Sydney, Melbourne, Adelaide, Perth and Brisbane. Art museum and gallery exhibitions display contemporary work from Australia and elsewhere. Paintings and sculpture addressing social issues are common themes. Aboriginal cooperatives exist in northern and central Australia and there are many women Aboriginal artists. Art galleries specializing in Aboriginal art have been established in the large Australian cities and Aboriginal work has received international recognition. ∎

This ancestral ▶ *figure, called a* pou tokomanawa, *is a sculpture in the round that served as a roof beam in a Maori meeting house. It was made in wood in about 1910. It portrays an individual ancestor. Usually devoid of decoration except for the ancestor's tattoos, such figures commonly display a three-fingered, splayed hand gesture across their stomachs or chests.*

The Maoris

Maoris are ethnic Polynesians who arrived by canoe around 800 to 900 A.D. and developed agriculture in New Zealand. Eventually, they became a warrior culture known for their fortified complexes. Today there are over 400,000 Maoris, making up twelve percent of the population, but only a third of the them use the Maori language. Many government-sponsored programs attempt to preserve aspects of Maori customs and culture and the Maori Arts and Crafts Institute trains young artists to a high standard. ■

This watercolor by H.G. Robley painted in ▶ *1864 is entitled* War Dance at Maketu Bay of Plenty. *It captures the fierceness and strength of the Maori tribes. The Maoris fought off the intruding westerners from 1840 when they first arrived. In 1872, the Maoris were overwhelmed by the British.*

By the mid-nineteenth century, Melbourne, on the southern coast, was the largest and richest Australian city. It was a cosmopolitan art center by the end of the century. One artist, Tom Roberts (1856–1931), returned to Melbourne in 1885 after studying in London. He explored the outback, producing many fine realist paintings of ordinary people and contemporary life. His work represented a second wave of immigrant self-discovery. Roberts and his Heidelberg School influenced Australian art and artists for decades.

Modern art movements appeared in Australia simultaneously with or soon after their beginnings in other parts of the world. Since the late 1970s, white Australian artists have recognized art forms, styles and traditions native to their country and begun to appreciate Australian subjects as the foundation of their work.

In New Zealand, the Maori population continued the art traditions of their Polynesian ancestors. Two factors governed Maori society: ancestor worship and class or social rank. All art was created for one's ancestors or for village chiefs and highborn individuals. The finest cloaks, ornaments, weapons, decorated houses and household items were made to dignify and distinguish this upper class.

To the Maoris, all knowledge is sent by the gods and all craftspeople were well respected members of society. Women worked with soft materials making garments, mats and baskets. Men made objects of wood, bone or stone. The Maoris believe that objects have a spiritual or magical component and that elaborate surface ornamentation is the essence of beauty. Maori ornamentation is widely practiced in three art forms: the canoe, the tribal meeting house and body art. The canoe was the most valued of tribal possessions. The prows and sterns had different types of decoration, including carvings of masks and exotic feathers.

Tribal meeting houses symbolized the body of an ancestor. They were built for hereditary chiefs and senior members of the village. Symbolic sculpture supported internal beams and rafters were richly painted with intricate, repetitive, curvilinear designs. These patterns

▲ *This is a portrait by the artist G. Lindauer of the Maori, Harawira Tatere, one of the chiefs of the Ngati Kahungunu. The tattoos on the chief's face are marks that indicate his status in society, that a member of a Maori tribe would be able to identify.*

Contemporary Art in New Zealand

Art museums display contemporary art in Auckland, Wellington, Dunedin and Christchurch. New Zealand artists produce representational and abstract art in all media. Unlike some artists in the west, New Zealand artists are generally not interested in shocking or political subjects. There is an active feminist community whose paintings accurately describe the position and interests of women. Many active crafts communities continue to produce innovative forms using native woods, wool and shells. ∎

This nineteenth century photograph shows a ▶
Maori family wearing traditional cloaks woven in flax, outside their meeting house. Maoris erected meeting houses as symbols of their ancestors.

also form the basis of tattoo designs.

Nearly every important Maori of rank had some form of facial tattoo. Spiral-shaped tattoos were made at ceremonies marking puberty. Some warriors also had tattooed buttocks and thighs. The practice of tattooing the entire face and most of the body lapsed in the nineteenth century. Before 1900 human skulls with richly ornamented faces were kept as cult objects.

Seventy years before the British colonists arrived, William Hodges (1744–97) sailed with the explorer Captain Cook (1729–79). Between 1772 and 1775, he produced views of the New Zealand landscape documenting Cook's circumnavigation.

Most colonial art between 1840 and 1900 was produced by amateurs. Professional artists from Europe arrived about 1900. Three were gifted painters and teachers. Petrus Van der Velden (1834–1913) produced Dutch genre scenes and local landscape paintings, James McLachlan Nairn (1859–1904) created Impressionist scenes and figure paintings and G.P. Nerli (1863–1926) painted accomplished portraits. Emphasis shifted away from amateur painting towards professionalism and painting in oils and pursuit of a European art education and experience abroad.

Many young artists moved to Paris and London. Nerli's pupil, Frances Hodgkins (1869–1947) arrived in London in 1900, and alternated between Europe and New Zealand for most of her life. In the early 1930s, she produced avant-garde paintings now in the major galleries of Great Britain, Australia and New Zealand.

Since World War II, New Zealand has mirrored Australian art trends. Auckland, Christ Church and Wellington all have thriving communities interested in Maori and western art.

20 Art of Indonesia and Oceania

▲ *This is Borobudur, the magnificent nine-tiered temple complex on Java that rises to 113 feet/34.5 meters. It was built from a grey volcanic stone called andesite in about 800 A.D. Its roughly 1.6 million stones were once covered in stucco and probably painted.*

Borobudur and the Volcano

Borobudur came to an abrupt end in 928 or 929, when the nearby volcano, Mount Merapi, erupted. The complex and the surrounding countryside were buried under deep layers of ash and lava. The explosion was so devastating that no further carved stone records were produced there until the fifteenth century. Later, Borobudur was ravaged by earthquakes and consumed by the jungle. The overgrown ruin was stumbled on in 1812 during British occupation of Indonesia. Expensive restoration work began in the late 1970s and was completed in 1983. ■

There are 1,500 stone relief carvings at ▶ *Borobudur, like this one of a woman carried by her two servants. The carvings tell stories of everyday life and tales from Buddhism.*

Religion in Indonesia

There are four major religions in Indonesian history, all brought to the islands by traders and missionaries. Buddhism came from India in the third century A.D. Hinduism arrived soon after, but not until the ninth century did it have many followers. Islam became important after the sixteenth century. In the seventeenth century, Christian missionaries followed western traders. Today eighty-eight percent of the population is Muslim, ten percent is Christian and the rest Buddhist or Hindu. Indonesia has the world's largest Muslim population. ■

The major focus of Indonesian art production has centered on the island of Java. Indian traders arrived in southeast Asia between the fifth and seventh centuries A.D., bringing with them Buddhism and Hinduism. In the next 200 years, native artists and craftspeople adopted Indian styles, yet created buildings and art forms in a purely Indonesian style.

The major Buddhist temple complex, at Borobudur, central Java, was begun in the eighth century. In 856, soon after the complex was completed, the Buddhist rulers of Borobudur were overthrown by Hindus. Borobudur was abandoned and replaced by the Hindu Prambanam complex, built between 900 and 930. Like Borobudur, it has been the victim of severe earthquakes and today is a combination of restored and ruined stupas, shrines and courtyards.

Islam arrived in Indonesia from western India in about 1527. Mosque

Indonesian Crafts

In addition to the rich textile tradition, Indonesia produces an extensive range of crafts. These include gold and silver earrings, necklaces and crowns for weddings and special ceremonies, ceramic and carved wooden figures that bring good luck for the rice harvest, carved bone and horn containers for storing medicines and puppets for use in traditional Hindu storytelling. ■

◀ *These Indonesian painted, wooden figures of* Dewi Sri, *the rice goddess (right) and* Sadono *(left), her consort, are traditionally placed near a bed in homes in Java. It is thought that they bring prosperity and fertility to the household.*

The Philippines

The Republic of the Philippines is made up of more than 7,000 islands in the western Pacific. Since prehistoric times it has been on the migratory path of the Chinese, Indians, Indonesians, Micronesians and Malaysians. It has not only an indigenous art culture but also western-influenced art since Spanish colonization in the sixteenth century. The native art forms include small wooden sculptures used in ancestor worship, baskets, mats and textiles with geometric patterns and brightly colored embroidery. ■

construction began to accommodate the growing Muslim population.

Exquisite textiles are Indonesia's most famous art form, recognized throughout the world. The two major types are known as ikat and batik. Ikat is a finely woven, tie-dyed form of wool or silk. Before weaving, its threads are bundled tightly with string and then dyed.

Batik is created using what is called a wax-resist process. First, wax is applied to a bleached piece of cloth. Once the waxed pattern has cooled and hardened, the cloth is dyed. When it dries the wax is removed. The undyed portions of the cloth will reveal the batik artist's design. Batik is produced on Java and Sumatra, less often on the outer islands.

Twentieth century Indonesian art reflects the Dutch colonial influence in batik designs with western floral patterns. Western painting techniques were also adopted. Artists often used the harsh brushstrokes and aggressive forms of German Expressionism to communi-

◀ *The sultan rulers of Java had their own, private batik designs. This late nineteenth century cotton design from Yogyakarta would have been worn only by royalty.*

This painting in acrylic shows ▶ *images of everyday life on the island of Bali. A woman collects water (bottom left). Another woman enters a village shrine (center left) and a man works in the terraced rice fields (center right). This was painted by an unidentified artist from the Peasant Painters' School for young people in Penestan, on Bali.*

Ancestral Poles

The Asmat people of southwest New Guinea carve striking poles called *bisj* poles. They resemble North American Indian totem poles. They are placed near

the houses of warriors honored in ceremonial rituals. The poles are elaborately carved with two or three large human figures and many smaller ones. ■

◄ *These tall* bisj *poles are each carved from a single tree trunk.*

Rapanui Figures

Materials available for arts and crafts were hard to obtain on the remote island of Rapanui in eastern Polynesia. This restricted the production of art, but monumental stone figures, some more than sixty feet/eighteen meters high and weighing almost twenty tons, were carved in tufa, a soft easily-worked form of volcanic stone quarried nearby. We do not know what these colossal figures represent. ■

▲ *The Rapanui figures have simple bodies, that make their mask-like heads seem overpowering. They were made in the seventeenth century or possibly earlier.*

cate their trauma following Japanese occupation during World War II.

After independence in 1949, artists began to integrate western techniques to produce enlivened and colorful paintings of contemporary life. There is an active art colony in Ubud on the island of Bali. The batik technique has also been used in creating batik paintings.

The Pacific islands of Oceania are usually divided into Melanesia, Micronesia and Polynesia. Their inhabitants share some social conventions and beliefs and have some unique ones. Traditional societies were based on farming, fishing and an extensive exchange system. The materials exchanged included wood, stone and bone for carvings, with flowers, seeds, shells and feathers added for decoration. The tools used were made from stone, bone or shell.

Objects from Oceania may be appreciated as art forms but they were also symbols of power or prestige, representing the owner's social rank. They may also have served as temporary homes for spirits. Artists decorated masks, canoes and battle shields. Immediate inspiration from the surroundings was critical in determining the final product. These art forms were never intended to be permanent. Many were destroyed soon after use.

Melanesian art was produced as a means of communication, addressing man's relations with his surroundings, ancestors and gods. The prestige of a person is established both by what he or she is seen to possess and by what is given to others. Exchange ceremonies often involve short speeches, dancing and body decoration, all activities that traditionally accompanied spirit worship ceremonies.

New Guinea is the major focus of art production in Melanesia. The Sepik River region produces many of the most famous Oceanic carvings. There are free-standing figures of human beings and animals

Island Groups

Melanesia comprises the islands of New Guinea and those eastward to Fiji, including the Solomon Islands and Vanuatu. The oldest settlements in New Guinea date back 40,000 years. Micronesia is the region north of Melanesia. This four-island group is east of the Philippines and southeast of Japan, and includes the Caroline Islands and the Marshall Islands. They were settled from west to east about 2,000 to 3,000 years ago. Polynesia is the most eastern of the island groups. It spreads over vast areas of the Pacific from Hawaii in the north, through the Marquesas and the Cook Islands in the east, to New Zealand in the south. The western portions of Polynesia were also settled about 3,000 years ago. ■

The Art of Hawaii ____

Bark cloth, ceremonial clothing and carved wooden figures are all made with exceptional craftsmanship in Hawaii. Decorative bark cloth produced in Hawaii is renowned for its fine quality. Cloaks, capes and helmets are decorated with representative images of gods. The helmets consist of bright red and yellow feathers attached to a fiber and wicker framework. ■

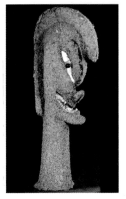

◀ *This image of a Polynesian god was made in Hawaii from feathers, human hair and shells. It dates from the eighteenth century. The god's teeth are made of polished dog's teeth.*

Warriors on the Caroline Islands, like Chief Dapoy of Gagil, pictured below, tattoo their bodies with geometric shapes that are meant to disarm and disorient their opponents. ▼

with large heads, stunted bodies and faces with extremely long narrow noses. Dance drums, hooks, boat prows and shields are also carved. The work is typically painted with swirling curves and oval shapes, decoration that floats across all surfaces.

Polynesian arts and crafts include carved ceremonial clubs, decorative wooden furniture, finely woven mats and *tapa*. *Tapa* is made by beating specially prepared and soaked tree bark to the desired size and shape, different on each island. On Fiji, Tahiti and Samoa, it was often decorated with printed or stamped geometric designs. On Hawaii, small, carved, bamboo printing sticks were used to create precise designs and colored particles were beaten into the *tapa* for extra decoration.

Body art, in the form of decorative clothing, jewelry, tattoos and scarification is another Oceanic art form. Such decorations indicate one's place in the community. Tattoos are an art form throughout Polynesia and parts of Micronesia. Tattoo artists are highly respected, the equal of sculptors and wood carvers. The English word tattoo is derived from the Polynesian word *tatau*. Tattoo art reached its height on the Marquesas Islands where a man's entire body was covered in tattoos. Scarification involves making carved incisions or designs in the skin that heal with prominent scars. Human flesh was an artistic medium for communicating symbolic meanings in Polynesian society.

Tapa or Bark Cloth _____

Before the discovery of woven textiles, people wore clothing made from animal skins or tree bark. Polynesian bark-cloth is called *tapa*, the Polynesian word for cloth, made from mulberry bark. It was produced for trade and as special gifts. Chiefs and island rulers collected many rolls of *tapa* as a symbol of their wealth and prestige. *Tapa* production almost died out during French colonization in the nineteenth century, but continued uninterrupted on the Marquesas Islands. ■

▲ *A Samoan craftsman decorates a piece of* tapa *with intricate designs. Decorative pieces of* tapa *are sometimes exchanged with tourists for goods.*

Bibliography

Baker, Joan Stanley. *Japanese Art*. New York and London: Thames and Hudson, 1984.

Barnard, Nicholas. *Arts and Crafts of India*. London: Conran Octopus, 1993.

Blurton, T. Richard. *Hindu Art*. London: British Museum Press, 1992.

Brend, Barbara. *Islamic Art*. London: British Museum Press, 1994.

Fisher, Robert E. *Buddhist Art and Architecture*. New York and London: Thames and Hudson, 1993.

Fraser-Lu, Sylvia. *Handwoven Textiles of Southeast Asia*. New York and Oxford: Oxford University Press, 1992.

Lee, Sherman. *A History of Far Eastern Art*. 4th ed. Englewood, N.J.: Prentice–Hall, 1982.

McCullough, Alan and Susan. *Encyclopedia of Australian Art*. London: Herbert Press, 1994.

Rawson, Philip. *The Art of Southeast Asia*. New York and London: Thames and Hudson, 1990.

Richter, Anne. *Arts and Crafts of Indonesia*. New York and London: Thames and Hudson, 1993.

Thomas, Nicholas. *Oceanic Art*. New York and London: Thames and Hudson, 1995.

Tredger, Mary. *Chinese Art*. New York and London: Thames and Hudson, 1991.

Glossary

authoritarian The word that describes someone who demands absolute obedience.

betel A nut and leaf chewed for its stimulating effects.

Brahma The Hindu god of the world spirit or world soul with no shape or tangible form; the essence of the universe and the individual soul.

Buddha A person who has obtained complete enlightenment, free of suffering, ignorance and desire. Buddha is also the historical founder of Buddhism.

calligraphy A beautiful form of handwriting.

capital The decorative element at the top of a column.

chaitya The Sanskrit word meaning "sanctuary." Also the rectangular meeting hall for early worshippers of Indian Buddhism.

Communism A revolutionary socialist theory of communal ownership of property in which all citizens work toward common goals of the state. It was first attempted in Russia in 1917 and adopted in China in 1949.

fresco A type of painting made on wet plaster.

genre Pictures which represent ordinary people and everyday life.

glaze A coating applied to ceramics before firing for decoration and sometimes to make the ceramic non-porous.

gouache A form of watercolor in which the pigments are bound in glue.

Khmer The Cambodian people or the period in their history between the ninth and fifteenth centuries.

lama A high priest of Tibetan Buddhism.

mausoleum A large tomb.

meditation Deep thought or contemplation.

mihrab A decorative indentation in the wall of the mosque indicating the direction towards Mecca.

patina A film on the surface of an object caused by oxidation.

perspective A way of representing objects or figures in a work of art to show relative distance or depth.

sarong A length of cloth worn by men and women in Malaysia, Indonesia and Oceania.

Shah The title of hereditary monarchs of Persia and Iran.

Social Realism A style of art that depicts things as they are to make social or political comment.

stucco Ornamental plaster work.

stupa A memorial tomb of the Buddha, sometimes containing sacred relics; in India a hemisphere on top of a rectangle.

sultan A ruler or king of a Muslim country.

ukiyo-e A Japanese term meaning "pictures of the floating world" that describes the prints and paintings produced to capture daily life, particularly in the theater and entertainment district.

Photo Credits

Asian Art Museum of San Francisco: 17

The Asia Society, New York: 46 bottom

Trustees of the British Museum: 12 top, 59 top left

Chao Sam Phraya National Museum in Ayutthaya, Thailand: 47 bottom right

Charles Doherty: 34 left

courtesy Galerie Lā Vong, Hong Kong: 50 left

Hara Museum of Contemporary Art, Tokyo: 43 bottom

House of Handicrafts, Bangkok: 50 left

Imperial Museum, Beijing: 27 bottom

India Office Library, London: 20 bottom left

courtesy Mausoleum of Tamerlane, the Gur Emir, Samarkana: 11 bottom

Museum of Decorative Arts, Frankfurt: 28 bottom left

Museum of Fine Arts, Boston: 21 left

Museum of Fine Arts, St. Petersburg, Florida: 15 bottom

Museum of New Zealand Te Papa Tongarewa, Wellington, New Zealand: 54 bottom, 55 top

National Gallery of Victoria, Australia: 53 bottom left and right

National Museum, Phnom-Penh: 49 top

Oriental and Indian Office Collections, The British Library: 22 right

Otago Museum, Dunedin, New Zealand: 54 top

Peasant Painters' School, Penestan, Bali: 57 right

Private Collection: 10, 12 bottom, 13 right, 14, 15 top, 16 top, bottom right and left, 19 top, 21 right, 22, 23 top and bottom, 24 top, bottom left and right, 25 top, bottom left and right, 26 left, top and bottom right, 27 top, 28 top left and right, 29 top and bottom, 30 top and bottom, 31 top and bottom, 32 left and right, 33 left and right, 34 right, 35 left and right, 43 bottom, 46 top, 47 top left and right, 48 left, top and bottom right, 49 bottom, 51 top and bottom, 52 top and bottom, 53 top left, 55 bottom, 56 top and bottom, 57 top and bottom left, 58 top and bottom, 59 bottom left and right

Smithsonian Institution, Freer Gallery of Art, Washington, D.C.: 18

Sotheby's: 11 top, 20 right

Tokyo Museum: 43 top

Victoria and Albert Museum: cover, 13 top and center left, 19 bottom, 20 top left, 39 bottom, 42

Index

Aborigines, 52-54
Ajanta, 14, 46
Akbar the Great, 18-20
ancestor worship, 26, 52, 54, 58
Angkor Wat/Angkor period, 47-49
Aryans, 14-15
Asmats, 57
Aung San Suu Kyi, 47
Australia, 52-54
Ayatollah Khomeini, 13
Ayutthaya School, 47

Babur, 18
Bada Shanren, 32
Bali, 57-58
bamboo/bamboo carving, 29, 45, 47, 51, 59
Bangkok School, 47
bark cloth/painting, 52, 59
baskets, 51, 54, 57
batik, 51, 57, 58
Bayon, 49
betel, 47
Bhaktapur, 24
bisj poles, 57
bodhisattva, 15, 37, 44
body painting, 52, 54, 58-59
Bok, Sin Yun, 45
bone carving, 54, 57-58
book illustrations, 12, 19-20
Borobudur, 56
British East India Company, 18, 22
British Raj period, 22-23
bronze, 11, 14, 18-19, 24-26, 32, 37, 44, 47, 49
Buddha, 14-16, 28, 37, 39, 46-47, 50
Buddhism, 11, 14-15, 17-19, 24-26, 28-29, 31, 36-39, 44, 46-49
    Burmese, 46
    Cambodian, 48-49
    Chinese, 26, 28-29, 31
    Indian, 11, 14-15, 17-19
    Indonesian, 56
    Japanese, 36-39
    Korean, 44
    Khmer, 49
    Nepalese/Tibetan, 24-25
    Thai, 47
Bukhara, 11, 13
Burma, 15, 17, 33, 46-47
Byzantine Empire, 12

calligraphy, 12-13, 21, 29-30, 33, 37, 39, 51
Cambodia, 47, 48-49, 50
canoes, 54, 58
Caroline Islands, 58, 59

carpets, 10-13, 19-20, 22, 25, 35
caste system, 14
caves, 14, 28, 52
celadon, 29, 44, 45
ceramics, 10, 12, 14, 27-29, 39-40, 44, 57
Ceylon, 15, 46
chaitya, 15
Champa kingdom, 48, 49-50
Ch'ang-an (Xian), 28, 37
Chang Dai Chien, 35
Chiang Kai Shek, 35
China, 26-35, 37, 42-46, 49, 57
Chinese characters, 27, 31, 36, 44
Chinnery, George, 33
Christianity, 18, 40, 50, 56
Chu, Asai, 43
Cixi, Empress, 32
cloisonné, 31
Communism, 13, 34-35, 45, 50
Condor, Charles, 53
Confucius, 26
Confucianism, 26, 44
Corot, Jean-Baptiste Camille, 43
Cultural Revolution, 34-35

Dalai Lama, 25
dance, 17, 37-38, 49, 58, 59
Datong, 28
Dayal, Lin Din, 22
delftware, 31
Dharmapala, 24
Dongson culture, 49
dragons, 15, 31, 33
dreamtime, 52
Dvaravati School, 47

earthenware, 26, 28, 36
Easter Islands (Rapanui), 58
Edo (Tokyo), 41-43
embroidery, 20, 33, 35
enameling, 20, 31

feathers, 58-59
Forbidden City, Beijing, 32, 34
furniture, 31, 33, 43, 59

Gandhara, 15
Gandhi, Mahatma, 23
Ganesha, 17
gardens, 21, 28, 31, 32, 37, 40
Gauguin, Paul, 23
gems/jewels, 10, 13, 22, 36, 44
Genghis Khan, 11, 30
glass, 10, 19-20, 43-44

gold, 10-11, 25, 27, 30, 37, 39-40, 44, 47, 51, 57
Great Wall of China, 27
Gupta Period, 16-18, 46

Hall of Supreme Harmony, Beijing, 32
Hamza-Nama, 19-20
Hawaii, 58-59
Han Dynasty, 27-28
Heian (Kyoto), 37-38
Heidelberg School, 53
Hideyoshi, Toyotomi, 40-41
Hinduism, 14, 16-19, 24, 47-49, 56
Hirohito, Emperor, 43
Hiroshige, Ando, 41
Hiroshima, 43
Hodges, William, 55
Hodgkins, Frances, 55
Hokusai, Katsushika, 41
Hong Kong, 33
Hsiao Yun-ts'ung, 30
Hui-Zong, 29
Hyderabad, 22-23

ikat, 50-51, 57
Imari porcelain, 40
India, 14-23, 25, 28, 33, 46, 48, 57
Indian miniatures, 19-20
Indonesia, 10, 17, 47, 51
Iran, 13
Isfahan, 10, 12-13
Islam, 10-12, 18-19. 51, 56
Ismail Shah, 13
Isnik, 12-13
ivory, 10, 20

jade, 27, 35, 44
Jahangir, 18, 20-21
Japan, 34, 36-45
Japan Art Academy, 42
Java, 56, 57
Jayavarman II, 48
Jayavarman VII, 48
Jesuits, 18, 40
jewelry, 20, 29, 44, 57, 59
Jomon, 36

kabuki theater, 41
Kamakura, 38
Kangxi, 32
Kashmir, 22-23
Kathmandu, 24
Khitans, 32
Khmer culture, 47-48
kimono, 39
kite making, 51
Kogyo, Tsukioka, 42
Koran, 10, 21

Korea, 10, 13, 21, 37, 40, 44-45
Koryo period, 44-45
Kublai Khan, 11
Kyanzittha, King, 46
Kyongju, 44
Kyoto (Heian), 36-37, 40-41

lacquer, 20, 27, 30-31, 33, 37, 41, 46-47
Lao Tse, 26
Laos, 49-51
Les Kwan Yew, 51
Lhasa, 25
Li Hua, 34
Lindauer, G., 55
Lopburi, 47
Luang Prabang, 50
Luoyang, 28
Lycett, Joseph, 53

Mahabharata, 17
Malaysia (Malay Peninsula), 10, 17, 47, 51, 57
Manchus/Manchuria, 32, 34, 43
manuscript illumination, 11-12, 19-20, 24
Mao Zedong, 34-35
    Little Red Book, 34
Maori, 54
Maori Arts and Crafts Institute, 54
Marquesas Islands, 58, 59
Marshall Islands, 58
masks, 24, 37, 39, 54, 58
Mayo School of Arts, 23
McCubbin, Frederick, 53
Meiji period, 42
Melanesia, 58
Merv, 11
Mesopotamia, 14
metalwork,
    Chinese, 26-27, 31
    Indian, 19-20
    Japanese, 39, 41
    Korean, 44
    Middle Eastern/Persian, 11-12
    Tibetan, 25
Micronesia, 57-59
mihrab, 10
Ming Dynasty, 30-31
Mohammed, Prophet, 10
Mohammed Reza, 12-13
Momoyama period, 40
Mon, 46-47
Mongols/Mongolia, 11-12, 27, 30, 44, 46
mosaics, 10-11
mosques, 10-12, 19

Mount Fuji, 41
Mount Meru, 15, 49
muezzin, 10
Mughal period, 18-21
Muramachi period, 39
music, 17, 49, 59
Myanmar, 46

Naash, Jamil, 23
Nagasaki, 43
Nairn, James McLachlan, 55
Nara, 37, 38
National Palace Museum, Taipei, 34
Nepal, 24-25
Nerli, G. P., 55
New Guinea, 58
New Zealand, 54-55, 58
Newars, 24
Nihonga, 42
No masks, 39
Noland, Sidney, 53

Oceania, 58-59
Ohura, Nobuyuki, 43
oil painting, 13, 23, 34-35, 42-43, 50, 53, 55
Opium Wars, 33
Ottoman Empire, 12

Pagan, 46
painting:
    Australian, 52-54
    Burmese, 46
    Chinese, 28-30, 32-35, 51
    Hong Kong, 33
    Indian, 17-23
    Indonesian, 57-58
    Japanese, 36-42
    Korean, 45
    Macao, 33
    Malaysian, 51
    Middle Eastern/Persian, 11-12, 19, 21
    Nepalese, 24
    New Zealander, 55
    Oceanic, 59
    Singapore, 51
    Thai, 47
    Tibetan, 24-25
    Vietnamese, 50-51
Pakistan, 10, 15, 18, 23
Parvati, 18
Patan, 24
Peacock Throne, 13
People's Republic of China, 34-35

Persia, 10-14, 18-19, 31
Persian miniatures, 12, 19, 21
Philippines, 57-58
photography, 22
Pol Pot, 49
Polynesia, 54, 58-59
porcelain,
    Chinese, 10, 12, 29, 31-33, 35
    Japanese, 40
    Korean, 44-45
    Middle Eastern/Persian, 11, 13
Potala, Lhasa, 25
pottery,
    Chinese, 26
    Indian, 14
    Japanese, 36, 40, 45
    Korean, 44-45
    Middle Eastern/Persian, 12
pou tokomanawa, 54
Prambanam, 56
puppets, 57
Pyu, 46

Qianlong, 32
Qin Dynasty, 26-27
Qin Shi Huangdi, 26-27
Qing Dynasty, 32-33

Rajput, 21
Ramayana, 17, 51
Rapanui (Easter Islands), 58
relief carvings,
    Burmese, 46
    Cambodian, 48-49
    Indian, 15, 17-18
    Indonesian, 65
    Laotian, 51
    Middle Eastern/Persian, 10
Revolutionary Realism, 35
Roberts, Tom, 53-54
Robley, H. G., 54
rock painting, 52
Russo-Japanese War, 42

Safavid Dynasty, 12
Samanids, 11
Samarkand, 11-13
Samoa, 59
samurai, 38-39, 42
Sanchai, 16
Sanskrit, 14, 17
Sarawak, 51
Saudi Arabia, 10
scarification, 59
screens, 36, 39-41

sculpture, 14-19, 24, 27, 37-38, 44, 46-47, 49-51, 54, 58-59
    Australian, 34
    Burmese, 46
    Cambodian, 49
    Chinese, 27
    Indian, 14-19, 24
    Japanese, 37-38
    Khmer, 49-50
    Korean, 44
    Laotian, 51
    Nepalese, 24
    Oceanic, 58-59
    Thai, 47
    Vietnamese, 50-51
Sepik River, 58
Shah Abbas I, 10, 12
Shah Jahan, 18, 20-21
Shakti, 17
Shang period, 26, 49
Shanghai, 34
shawls, 22, 47
shells, 55, 58-59
Sher Gil, Amrita, 23
Shikibu, Lady Murasaki, 36
Shintoism, 36
Shiraz, 12
Shiva, 16-18, 49
shoguns, 38, 40-42
Shunzhi, 33
Siddhartha Gautama, 14
silk, 10, 13, 24, 31, 33, 38-39, 47, 50-51
Silk Road, 10-11, 28-29, 31
silver, 10-11, 25, 30, 39, 44, 47, 51, 57
Singapore, 51
Sino-Japanese War, 33
Social Realism, 34
Solomon Islands, 58
Song Dynasty, 28-30
songket, 51
Spice Islands, 22
Sri Lanka, 15, 46
Srivijaya School, 47
stele, 46
stone carving/engraving, 14-17, 19-20, 28, 44, 46-49, 52, 54, 56, 58
Streeton, Arthur, 53
stupas, 15-16, 24, 46, 56
Sukhothai School, 47
Summer Palace, Beijing, 32
Surya, 14
swords, 39

Tahiti, 59

Taiwan, 34
Taj Mahal, Agra, 21
Takanobu, Fujiwara, 38
Tamerlane, 11-12
Tang Dynasty, 28-30, 37
Taoism, 26, 28-29
tapa, 59
tattoos, 54-55, 59
tea/tea ceremony, 31, 39-41
temples, 16, 18-19, 28, 31, 37-38, 46-49
terracotta, 14, 26, 28
textiles, 20, 22, 25, 30-33, 47, 50-51, 55, 57, 59
Thailand, 15, 46-47, 49, 51
thangkas, 25
theater/drama, 17, 39, 41, 43
The Tale of Genji, 36
Tiananmen Square, Beijing, 35
Tibet, 24-25, 27
tiles, 10-13, 27, 46

Ubud, 57
ukiyo-e, 41, 43
Unified Silla period, 44
Unkei, 38
Uzbekistan, 13

Van der Velden, Petrus, 55
Vanuatu, 58
Vedas, 14, 17
Viet Dung, 51
Vietnam, 28, 33, 48-51
Vietnamese wars, 50-51
Vishnu, 16-17

weapons, 27, 38-39, 54, 58-59
women artists, 33, 50-51, 55
wood carving, 15, 20, 24-25, 27, 37-38, 47, 51, 53-55, 57-59
woodblock prints, 34, 41-44
Wright, Frank Lloyd, 42

Xian (Ch'ang-an), 26

Yagoi, 36
Yokoo, Tadanori, 43
yamato-e, 37-38
Yogyakarta, 57
Yoritomo, Minamoto no, 38
Yuan Dynasty, 11, 29-30
Yuan Yunsheng, 35

Zen Buddhism, 37-40, 42-43
Zenderoudi, Hossein, 13
Zhou period, 26, 49
Zubir, Sharifa Fatimah, 51